A Father's Journey of
Grief and Recovery

Letters to Stephen

JAMES TAYLOR

Northstone

Editor and photographer: Michael Schwartzentruber
Cover design: Lois Huey-Heck
Consulting art director: Robert MacDonald

Northstone Publishing Inc. is an employee-owned company, committed to caring for the environment and all creation. Northstone recycles, reuses and composts, and encourages readers to do the same. Resources are printed on recycled paper and more environmentally friendly groundwood papers (newsprint), whenever possible. The trees used are replaced through donations to the Scoutrees For Canada Program. Ten percent of all profit is donated to charitable organizations.

Permissions:

Canadian Cataloguing in Publication Data
Taylor, James, 1936-
    Letters to Stephen

    Includes bibliographical references.
    First ed. has title: Surviving death: healing and growing through grief.
    ISBN 1-55145-054-2

1. Grief. 2. Bereavement—Psychological aspects. I. Title. II. Title: Surviving death.
BF575.G7T39 1996   155.9'37   C96-910373-5

Published under license from Wood Lake Books by
Northstone Publishing Inc.

Printed in Canada by
Best Book Manufacturers

Northstone

Table of Contents

Acknowledgments

As I write this, it's been ten years since our son Stephen died. That's a long time in which to be working on a book.

Many people have helped shape this book. The first of those was Stephen himself, to whom I wrote a series of letters after his death.

I sent copies of a few of those letters to my business partner in Wood Lake Books, Ralph Milton. His assurance that what I had written to a dead son was not just demented drivel, but had some significant insights into life and faith as well as grief, encouraged me to keep those letters on file.

When I finally got around to using those letters as the basis for this book, I sent early drafts of half a dozen chapters to a number of people. Some were working associates: Ralph Milton again, David Cleary, Tim Faller, Mike Schwartzentruber, and Stephen's sister and our daughter, Sharon Taylor. They too encouraged me to proceed to a complete book.

Finally, I sent a complete book manuscript to a number of additional people whom I knew had passed through – or were still passing through – their own shadowed valleys of grief: Darryl Auten, Nenke Jongkind, Grant Kerr, Jan Kraus, Anne Ng, June Stevenson, and Howard Zurbrigg. All provided valuable feedback, often despite their own pressing emotional and professional agendas. So did Sharon, again, and my father, Bill Taylor. Jan Chapman and Kari Milton gave detailed critiques, often catching fine points that I, and editor Mike Schwartzentruber, had overlooked.

Every comment had its impact on the final shape of this book. I'm deeply grateful for the time – and yes, for the emotional support – that I have received from so many people and that has made this book possible.

– Jim Taylor

Preface

Someone you love has died. Or something you love has died: a relationship, a sense of belonging, a career, an ideal.

In that loss, a part of you died. You gave your heart to that person, your soul to that cause. When they die, so does part of you. You will never be the same again.

You have survived a death. Now you have to learn how to live when an essential part of you is missing. You have been maimed – the damage to you is just as real as losing a limb in an accident, or losing control of part of your body in a stroke. But you are more than a body. You are also mind and spirit, a complex web of relationships and accomplishments. And part of that complex web has been broken. Now you have to learn how to live again, without the person, the ambition, the dream, that died.

At this point in your painful rebirth, assurances that new life is possible won't mean much to you. Even if a personal resurrection is possible, you may not feel that it is worth having. You'd rather have the old life back again. But that's no longer possible. Despite the wonders of medical science, deaths cannot be reversed. They can only be survived.

You can survive this experience of death, and come out on the other side – the same person but different, the same person but changed.

This book is about what's happening to you. If it isn't happening to you right now, it's happening to someone you care about: a spouse, a friend, a child... I know what it's like. I have been there. So have many others.

To you, struggling to survive the death of life as you knew it, I dedicate this book.

Introduction

Neither to Regret nor Forget

On May 18, 1983, I went to Michelle Breakwell's funeral.

Our son Stephen decided not to come with me. Like Michelle, he had cystic fibrosis, an incurable hereditary illness that affects the lungs and the digestive system. He didn't feel very energetic that day. So I went alone.

Michelle's parents sat in the front pew of Bloordale United Church, one aisle over and half a dozen pews in front of me. I was surprised by their apparent composure. For 19 years, they had done everything that they could do to help their daughter stay alive. Now she was dead. And they were able to smile, to shake hands, to greet people warmly. Until the final hymn of the funeral. The second line of the second verse said, "...to our fathers in distress."

I'm sure that when the hymn was chosen, no one ever thought how that line might penetrate the defenses of a specific father in distress. Suddenly, Ken's head dropped, his shoulders heaved, and for a moment, he turned to his wife and sobbed.

Ken was not a close friend of mine; nor was Michelle a close friend of Stephen's. But we were acquaintances, through contacts at the camp for CF children, through the CF Foundation, and occasionally, through meetings when our children happened to be hospitalized for treatment at the same time. Several times over those years, I suddenly became aware that Ken's experience was also mine. In him, I saw myself.

At that funeral, I realized that his anguish would someday be mine. Some day it would be my turn to stand with Joan and our daughter Sharon, in the front pew of a church, grieving for a child who had died.

The time came sooner than any us of had expected.

Less than three months later, on August 6, Stephen died. A lung infection had flared up. In three days, he was gone. He was 21.

It's a painful thing when a child dies. William Sloane Coffin Jr., the minister of Riverside Church in New York, wrote in A.D. magazine after the death of his own son: "When parents die, as my own mother did recently, they take with them a large portion of the past. But when children die, they take away the future as well. That is what makes the valley of the shadow of death so incredibly dark and unending."

It is a painful thing when anyone – or anything deeply valued – dies. And only those who have been through it can begin to understand what it is like for those who survived that death.

Living with Unimaginable Loss

Heart-stopping loss is not limited to the death of a person. During the last few years, corporations and businesses have dumped many thousands of people onto the jobless trashpile. As irrevocably as death, these people have lost their incomes and their sense of self-worth. Though as a society we don't often recognize it, they go through grief just as my family did when Stephen died.

There are many causes for grief. The breakup of a marriage can be as traumatic as the loss of the same spouse to death. Divorce may even be worse – for a divorce can foster bitterness as well as regret.

Every individual loss affects others. Bill Howes was a stalwart member of our congregation. When his job came to an abrupt and unexpected end, many people in our congregation expressed sympathy. As weeks of unemployment grew into months, we continued to express concern and support for him.

One evening, after a meeting, Joan and I happened to be standing outside the church with Merle Howes, Bill's wife. "How's Bill doing?" we asked.

"Everyone asks how Bill's doing," Merle retorted. "Bill's doing fine. Why doesn't anyone ask how I'm doing? This is hard on me too, you know."

The Principal Source

In writing this book, I have drawn on the experiences that others have shared with me. I have also done considerable reading, planned and unplanned, on the subject.

But my principal source has been my own experience.

Stephen's sister Sharon and his mother Joan do not receive as much attention in these pages as he and I do. That's not because they were unimportant in the family – though in truth both their needs often took second place to Stephen's – but because this is the story of the impact that one person had on me. It is based on a personal relationship which has now ended.

For me, writing has always been a kind of therapy. Throughout my life, I have used writing as a way of working out my tensions, of figuring out what was happening to me. I wrote letters, I wrote diaries, I wrote articles. They dealt with facts. They also helped me uncover and examine the feelings and situations that were nibbling at the edges of my soul. The act of writing helped me make sense out of experiences and information which otherwise remained undigested and meaningless.

So in the days following Stephen's death, I turned, as usual, to the typewriter – actually, the computer lurking in my basement office. I wrote the story of his final days. In my journal, I wrote the beginnings of my own new life without him. And as time passed, I found myself writing letters to him.

At the time, I wondered if I might be going mad. Writing letters to a dead person is not a particularly normal thing to do. But whoever claimed that, in grief, we act normally?

In fact, what I did is not that unusual. At least one grief therapy program actually instructs mourners to write letters to the person who has died.

As the days passed, I found that writing letters to Stephen enabled me to get in touch with my own feelings better than any other method. I didn't have to put on a brave front. I didn't have to disguise my true emotions for fear of breaking down; nor did I have to soft pedal them to spare a listener unnecessary pain. Letters allowed me to focus my feelings, and to address those feelings to someone who understood. He had been through it himself – even more than I had. I had only lost a son; he had lost everyone.

Ten years later, those letters formed an invaluable record of my personal grief, and of the beginnings of change. So I have drawn upon them, whenever it seemed appropriate.

I have not used every letter. The last letter I have included was written right after our first Christmas without Stephen. I did not use any letters I wrote after that, because I don't think they add anything to understanding the symptoms of grief and the growth of healing.

The quotations from those letters appear much as I poured them out at the time. I have corrected spelling and punctuation; I have removed repetitions, and, occasionally, tidied up references for clarity. But I have not rewritten the letters themselves. What you see is what I wrote.

Please do not assume that because my grief in these letters is as raw as an open wound, I still feel that way. Yes, I still grieve. I always will. But I do not grieve with the intensity I once did. Only when someone else goes through a similar experience – when Lutheran pastor Ray Kirk's 15-year-old son Chris was killed crossing a road, for example – does the pain come back as sharply as ever. But the pain passes. In its place remains a deep gratitude for having been allowed to have a son who was also a friend, whose life I was privileged to share for 21 years. I do not regret those years any more than I regret having had friends in high school, in university, or in various jobs. Our paths may no longer cross, but I am grateful for the time when they did.

I do not regret, and I do not forget.

I exhume these letters not to parade my own grief, but in the hope that you may hear in them some echoes of your own experience. And so that, having heard some of your own sorrow, you too can move on without either regretting or forgetting.

Symptoms

"An astonishing number of people, I find, are not aware that grief has symptoms. They recognize grief only as that initial flood of tears or as shocked numbness. They certainly do not think of grief as a process, an unfolding experience that has certain predictable characteristics..."

The Symptoms of Grief

Over the past two decades, I have had more griefs than I like to remember. Stephen's was the major one. But during that period we also lost my mother and stepmother, Joan's father, my boss and mentor, a favorite cousin, five aunts, three uncles, and a dearly beloved 20-year-old cat, not to mention what I thought of as the best job in the world. I didn't always realize that these events had induced grief. In fact, it was often only when I recognized a symptom that I could identify grief as a cause.

An astonishing number of people, I find, are not aware that grief has symptoms. They recognize grief only as that initial flood of tears or as shocked numbness. They certainly do not think of grief as a process, an unfolding experience that has certain predictable characteristics.

Dr. Elisabeth Kübler-Ross, working with terminally ill patients, pioneered grief studies. She identified a recurring pattern of emotions:

1. Shock and denial
2. Anger
3. Bargaining
4. Depression
5. Acceptance

At times, I think that Dr. Kübler-Ross has been the most prophetic voice of the last half of this century. Many people have done things that have changed our lives – from the assassins of the Kennedys to the inventors of the microchip. But Dr. Kübler-Ross gave us a key, a talisman, that helps us understand how those changes affect us. The cycle that she identified applies, to some extent, to every significant change in life.

The cause doesn't matter. Death and illness bring about

grief. So do separation and divorce, firing and retirement, moving to a new home and moving to a new job.

The editor of a church magazine told me about her divorce. During the time of separation, she said, when it was clear there was no hope of salvaging the marriage, she often spent the whole evening sitting on her couch with her knees drawn up, wrapped up to her chin in a blanket, staring at nothing.

"It sounds almost as if you're mourning the death of your marriage," her therapist suggested.

In fact, the change need not be tragic at all. When two individuals marry, they do so (usually) with joy and with high expectations. But they also give up their independence. They replace personal ambitions with shared goals. They make sacrifices. They would never think of the process of adjustment as grieving – but they will experience many of the same symptoms.

The birth of a child is also a time of celebration. But the arrival of a new baby always changes the parents' lives. However much they may have wanted that child, however much they may adore it, it inevitably changes their sleeping habits, their leisure activities, their freedom, their sex lives, their disposable income.

To a greater or lesser extent, they too will experience some symptoms of grief.

The Auto Industry

The reaction of the American auto industry to government legislation in the 1970s offers a perfect illustration of grief at a societal level.

In the early 1970s, as a result of the first Middle Eastern oil crisis, the governments of both Canada and the United States imposed laws that required car makers to reduce pollutants and increase efficiency.

The first reaction of the industry was shock and rejection: "That's impossible! We can't do it."

That was followed closely by anger: "They can't do this to us!" The industry lobbied vigorously to change or overturn the legislation.

But the legislation stood. So they began bargaining: "Yes, we can do it, but it will take longer than you've allowed. Extend the deadlines." Or, "We can't do as much as you expect. Reduce the requirements."

That didn't work either. And the American auto industry sank into a deep slump from which it only began to recover in the mid 1980s.

While the American automakers huddled in depression, however, the Japanese and, to a lesser extent, the European car makers accepted the challenge. They started producing cars which were not only more fuel efficient and cleaner, but better built.

Today, the North American auto industry is building the best cars it has ever built. They are better designed, better engineered, better driving. They are safer.

But that could only happen once they had reached the stage of acceptance.

Two Typical Symptoms

Two quick examples might illustrate the symptoms of grief.

After I lost an important job promotion, I recognized occasional flashes of irrational rage rising within me. If a driver cut in front of me, I wanted to step on the gas instead of the brake, to crash into the back of his car to teach him a lesson. I didn't do it – but I wanted to.

After one of these episodes, I reflected long enough to realize that this anger was not normal, that it must be a symptom of something deeper. When I sought the underlying cause, I realized that I had been kidding myself. I had been telling people that I didn't really mind not getting a promotion. But my irrational anger told me that the promotion had mattered to me much more than I had been willing to admit.

On another occasion, I had a bitter verbal battle with a colleague. Disagreements are part of work. I've grown accustomed to them in more than 35 years of employment. But this time, I went home surrounded by a blue-grey fog. I think it was early summer. A slanting sun made the cloudless sky sparkle; trees flaunted their new leaves. Probably. I only remember a heavy wet blanket pressing me down into the car seat. Every emotion had drained, like water running out of a bathtub.

I sat in the driveway, without the energy to get out of the car. "I am so depressed," I said to myself.

Then I understood why. That fight had been the last gasp of denial that my job was coming to an end. In becoming aware of my depression, I also became aware of what I had to accept.

Anger and depression are two common symptoms of grief.

No Two the Same

Statistics can examine how several million people will vote; they can predict how many times out of a thousand a coin will come down heads or tails; they can define the average life expectancy of the North American male. But they cannot determine how you as one individual will vote, or how your next coin toss will come down, or whether you will be alive tomorrow.

In the same way, Dr. Kübler-Ross's five stages of grief provide marvelous insight into the behavior of people in general, but they cannot predict how any one person will react to grief.

Dr. Kübler-Ross also did her primary research with those who were themselves dying. They reached acceptance – if indeed they ever reached that stage – only to die.

But the people for whom I am writing, the people whose lives are devastated by change, have not died. Rather, they have *survived* a death: of a person, a relationship, a career, a concept, a belief. For them, death is not a conclusion, but a beginning. It is not something they look towards, but something they look back on – the event that precipitates a whole chain of symptoms. As a result, the bargaining phase that Dr. Kübler-Ross observed is either reduced or missing among survivors of a death – whatever that death may be.

That's a small but crucial difference. Dying people can do a lot of bargaining on the way to acceptance (again, assuming acceptance ever comes). They can say, "Spare me, and I'll never smoke again." Or drink alcohol, or work overtime, or rob banks. They can make promises: "I'll go to church every Sunday; I'll donate blood to the Red Cross; I'll give to the Heart Fund."

But how can a survivor bargain? They've already lost what they wanted to save. Very few people could bargain with God, with a straight face, that they'll go back to church if God will restore their dead grandmother to life. Especially if they have touched and held that grandmother's cold body, seen her coffin lowered into the ground, and accepted their share of her legacy.

So the survivors of death, loss, and change will not necessarily experience all of Dr. Kübler-Ross's stages. And they almost certainly won't experience them in order, like climbing a set of stairs: first shock and denial; then anger; then bargaining; then depression; and lastly acceptance.

If you're grieving, I can assure you that you will experience most of those feelings, at some time. But you may well experience anger and depression at the same time, contradictory though the two emotions seem. You will probably have accepted your loss long before you will recognize that a new you has emerged, like a butterfly from a chrysalis.

As C.S. Lewis commented in *A Grief Observed*, the book he wrote about surviving his wife's death, grief and sorrow are "not a state but a process." Grief will change you. Permanently.

There are no shortcuts through that process of grief. But during your grief, you can influence the kind of person who will emerge from the other side.

The Symptoms of Change

Children's stories, in church, often liken Jesus' resurrection to a caterpillar's transformation into a butterfly. I've felt increasingly dissatisfied with such stories. For the butterfly is not a new creature, a new creation. It's subject to exactly the same physical laws of heat and cold, of life and death, of gravity and hunger, as the caterpillar was. The butterfly's cells contain exactly the same genetic code as the caterpillar's. It has merely come out of its chrysalis in a different form.

As a symbol for resurrection, the butterfly fails. But as a symbol for survival, the butterfly works wonderfully. Those who survive some kind of death in their lives do go into a cocoon, and they do emerge different.

In that change, the survivors experience a number of very specific symptoms. Every book, every expert, in the field of grieving lists different sets of symptoms. There will probably never be universal agreement. My own research – based on both reading and experience – picks out these symptoms:

- Cold, clear, rationality – an unemotional objectivity.
- Constant reminders – when a person has died, seeing that person everywhere; when an ideal or an idea has died, finding references in everything.
- A compulsion to revisit places, events, associated with the loss.
- Anguish so overwhelming it becomes physical pain.
- Unpredictable mood swings.

- Absolute apathy – about money, about relationships, about responsibilities.
- Vulnerability – a sense of being defeated by little things you could have brushed off at any other time.
- A desire to escape – to another place, another time, especially to former years.
- Physical fatigue that cannot be overcome by dogged determination.
- Irrational lashing out at family members and friends, colleagues, and sudden rage at strangers.
- An obsession with honoring the memory of the past – often a need to write or make known, somehow, the story of the person, thing, or cause that has ended.
- Wallowing in memories that contribute to pain.
- Feelings of guilt – a recurring refrain of "if only..."
- Loss of personal goals and ambition.
- A sudden and unusual flowering of dreams.
- A desperate search for meaning.

In the chapters in the next section, I look at some of these symptoms in more detail. As you start to recognize some of your own symptoms, you will understand better how you are progressing through grief.

See Your Doctor First

If you recognize any of these symptoms – and provided they have no physical cause – you are probably experiencing some kind of grief. But do not – I repeat, *do not* – assume that grief alone adequately explains those symptoms.

Extreme tiredness could be grief. It could also be the result of jetting across too many time zones. But on the off-chance that it could be cancer, especially if it doesn't clear up soon, see your doctor.

Extreme apathy about financial matters, job responsibilities, or personal relationships could be grief. It could also be caused by anything from alcoholism to Alzheimer's Disease.

Wild and unpredictable mood swings could result from grief. Or they could be a brain tumor, or pathological mental illness. (Or, as a woman who read an early draft of this chapter commented, "It could be menopause!")

I don't want to induce panic – "If I'm not grieving, I must have cancer!" But neither do I want you to ignore symptoms that could be caused by something other than grief.

The key to grief-related symptoms is that they pass. They are temporary. Check with a doctor, a psychiatrist, a counselor if the symptoms last. In fact, check even if they don't last.

The Duration of Grief

I can't tell you how long grief symptoms should last. Some griefs can pass in a few hours, some in a few days. Some will take years.

Almost every book I have read on this subject underestimates the length of time that grief can affect you. Perhaps the most widely distributed book on grief is Granger E. Westberg's little volume, *Good Grief*, first published by Fortress Press in 1962. I suspect the book was written mainly for clergy and other care-givers. To my mind, it deals with only the early stages of grief. It seems to assume that once people have survived that initial torrent of emotions, they can look after themselves.

But that's only the beginning.

I have, sometimes, been tempted to say to people, "Shouldn't you be over this by now?" It took my own experience of grieving to sensitize me to how long grief can last.

September 20

Dear son,

The other morning, going to a meeting down at church house, I was listening to Peter Gzowski on the radio. No, I haven't started listening to your station – heavy metal rock was your stuff, and as far as I am concerned, it can stay yours! He had a woman talking about grief. "You do get over it though, don't you," Peter said comfortingly.

"No," she said, "you never do. It's always there. You just grow around it, and incorporate it into your new personality."

At a writing course I taught, a woman told me, during lunch, that she was a recent widow.

"How long ago did it happen?" I asked her.

"Five years ago," she replied.

I explained that I was working on this book. "And," I said, "I was curious to know how long you felt it took before you were over it."

"I don't think you are ever over it," she answered abruptly, and changed the subject.

Another woman consulted me about publishing her memoirs. She and her husband had been missionaries to China. Her husband had died, unexpectedly, on the ship taking them across the Pacific. One chapter of her memoirs described the trauma of arranging a funeral at sea, and of her decision to continue the work that they had jointly been commissioned to do, as a single mother with a young child.

"It must have been a terribly difficult time," I sympathized.

Although 50 years had passed, her eyes filled with tears. "It was not the kind of thing one spoke about," she said.

Transition to New Life

Grief need not be crippling. Whether it changes your life for the better or the worse depends entirely on what you choose to do with it.

A minister told me he once invited a man to take on a responsible position in the local church.

"Oh, I couldn't," the man replied. "I didn't tell you – but I killed my little girl a while ago; I backed the car over her one day, going to work." His grief was evident in his face.

"I'm so sorry," the minister apologized. "When did it happen?"

The man looked up with tear-streaked cheeks. "Twenty-three years ago," he said. "She would have been 26 next month."

That man allowed his grief to paralyze him. He chose to withdraw from life. But his experience could have made him more sensitive, more compassionate, more committed.

Our daughter Sharon became an only child a month before she left home for university. She had a difficult year. Moving from home into a university residence, developing new learning habits, finding new friends, after having just lost her older brother – none of these experiences made life easy for her.

Yet she found, during that year, that other students sought her out. They unburdened their souls about a mother diagnosed with cancer, about their parents divorcing, about cheating boyfriends.

"It's almost as if they know that I'm hurting too," Sharon theorized on a trip home. "Sometimes I wonder if a purpose of Stephen's death was to teach us how to listen to other people who are hurting."

You cannot restore whatever has died in your life. You can restore yourself. The healing, if it happens, happens to you.

Shock

Our son Stephen died in a hospital room at 11:17 on a Saturday night. I know the time exactly. I was holding his head up, so that he could more easily cough away the fluids gurgling in his chest. He tried to cough, took a breath, and failed to take a second breath.

"That's it," said Grant Kerr, who was with me, standing by Stephen's bed.

I remember thinking, "Someday I'll want to know when this happened." So I glanced at Stephen's clock radio, its dials glowing faintly orange on his bedside table. They showed 11:17.

Four of us had maintained a vigil around Stephen's bed through those final days and nights: my wife Joan, our daughter Sharon, Grant, and I. We clung together, the survivors of this shared tragedy, for comfort, in a group hug, a flood of tears. And then suddenly we were very calm. The tears dried up. We talked normally with the nurses, with the social worker who got out of bed to come to the hospital to counsel us.

It was after midnight when we drove home through darkened streets. And as we drove, we discussed the prostitute in her tight leather skirt standing on the corner, the possibility of sunshine the next day, the absence of normal traffic on the freeway at that hour.

We seemed so rational, so cool, so in control of ourselves.

Acts of Self-Preservation

The first reaction, after any serious loss, is a stunned normalcy. Your mind seems quite clear; you're not overwhelmed at all; you're quite capable of carrying on with everyday life.

Mark Twain lost his beloved daughter Susy at the age of 24. In *The Autobiography of Mark Twain* he wrote of that initial state of numbed disbelief:

It is one of the mysteries of our nature that a man, all unprepared, can receive a thunderstroke like that and live. There is but one reasonable explanation of it. The intellect is stunned by the shock and but gropingly gathers the meaning of the words. The power to realize their full import is mercifully wanting. The mind has a dumb sense of loss – that is all. It will take mind and memory months and possibly years to gather all the details and thus learn and know the whole extent of the loss.

Stories abound of people behaving quite calmly after serious accidents. A driver climbs out of a wrecked car and directs rescue workers. A freight train runs over a boy playing by the tracks; the boy calmly picks up his severed arm and carries it to the nearest hospital. A bomb blows open a soldier's abdomen; the soldier dispassionately studies his own guts. Ignoring her own burns, a mother rescues her child from a second-floor bedroom in a flaming house.

This response is, of course, the body's defense mechanism against overwhelming physical assault. It goes into shock.

Shock does not mean passing out, or fainting, or going into hysterics. Such reactions *reduce* the victims' chances of surviving the injury. They become helpless. Only those who can still react have a chance. They can move out of harm's way, avoid further injury, or begin treatment. So the body learns to shut down its pain centers, and to shut out all distractions except the most immediate concern – survival.

The pain, the fear, the weakness will come later. After her child is safe, the mother will feel her burns. After being picked up by medics, the soldier will pass out. After he gets home, the driver will collapse.

We have all seen – and probably joked about – children who skin a knee on the way home from school, but don't burst into tears until they reach their own front steps.

I don't think they're either faking or hiding their pain; their bodies simply repress reaction to the damage until they are safely out of danger.

I've been hurt playing competitive sports. Almost always, I was able to finish the game. Only then did I stiffen up, start shivering, and have to be helped home.

Brittle Strength

The same kind of thing can happen with other kinds of losses. An injury doesn't have to be physical to be real.

Our first response to Stephen's death was a kind of "hypersanity." In some ways, we were calmer, more collected, than the hospital ward's social worker, who came to help us.

For a day or two, we were kept busy: picking up relatives at the airport, arranging for the memorial service, contacting friends, notifying the lawyer, the insurance companies. Dozens of people came to our house to offer sympathy. Some brought food which we shared around; for others, we provided.

We chose to have mourners come to our home rather than to the artificial environment of a funeral "parlor." Hosting all those people can be an added burden during a time of severe stress. But in another sense, it begins to integrate the ordinary and mundane tasks of daily life with this wholly new, dramatically different reality.

On the surface, at least, we probably seemed more in command of our emotions than many of those who called on us.

Journal entry   August 9

We were all prepared for hordes of people to come.
They came in the evening, mostly from the Scouting association. The Venturers crew [Stephen's Scout-mates]
all showed up in good pants, white shirts, and ties – a
most remarkable expression of respect. Jeff Seligman even
wore a suit. Rob Scheutze and Gord Honor were in tears
as they came in the door.

   The boys didn't know what to do or to say; they
stood there in the hall, leaning against the wall, with eyes
the size of spaniels'.

Journal entry   August 10

Joan had her hair done in the afternoon, in preparation
for the memorial service. Anna was trimming her hair
when she heard about Stephen. She sobbed all the way
through the rest of the trimming, then put her head on
Joan's shoulder and cried and cried.

I've seen the same pattern over and over. After one funeral,
the widow stood on the sidewalk outside the funeral home,
laughing and joking with the many friends who had come
out to support her. Only the funeral parlor's sign overhead
identified this gathering as a time of mourning rather than
a festive event. She was sustained only by the brittle strength
of shock.

   The morning after Al Darbyshire died during a heart
by-pass operation, I met his widow and their three children
– Peter, Patrice, and Andrew – at the funeral director's office to help them make arrangements and choose a coffin.

Half an hour later, I realized, we were standing around, almost unemotionally, resting our elbows on the chosen coffin, discussing Andrew's choice of university and courses.

William Sargant, in his now dated but still insightful book *Battle for the Mind*, compared Pavlov's experiments on dogs with human reactions to shock. Most people identify Pavlov only with conditioning experiments. But those findings were only part of a much larger series of experiments on stress. "Depending on the type of nervous system and the amounts of stress," Sargant noted, "sooner or later the brains of both dog and man retreat into varying degrees of 'protective' inhibition and dysfunction." (p. 10–11)

Yet the apparent strength of this period of shock is deceptive. Like thin ice covering a bog, it can crack without warning, dropping you into the bottomless quagmire below.

After Stephen's death, we began telephoning friends and relatives. That night, late as it was, we called my father and Joan's mother, out west. They seemed more shaken by the news than we were. The next morning, my first call was to Bob Little, who has been like a brother to me for 35 years.

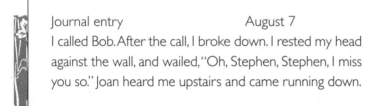

Journal entry   August 7
I called Bob. After the call, I broke down. I rested my head against the wall, and wailed, "Oh, Stephen, Stephen, I miss you so." Joan heard me upstairs and came running down.

The Compulsion to Verbalize

That sudden unpredictable breakdown, that sudden collapse from calm-cool-and-collected to utterly helpless, makes many people fear they're going crazy, losing their minds. In one sense, they are. Sometimes, at speaking engagements, I refer to grief as a form of temporary insanity; I see people all through the audience nod their heads. A person going through grief is certainly not "normal" – whatever that may be.

But the effects are temporary – that's the difference between grief and genuine mental illness. You will get over it.

The greatest need anyone has in this period of shock is an opportunity to talk. Despite their apparent rationality, one event dominates every thought. Only by talking about it, by talking about it over and over until they get tired of talking about it, will that event recede into perspective with the rest of life.

Journal entry   August 7

The Littles came around in the early afternoon, and stayed for several hours, long enough for us to get past talking about the tragedy and to start talking about normal things.

Then just as they left, Brian and Carol Jeffs called, to say that they were making hamburgers, and they thought that they would like to come over and cook them on our barbecue. Again, we sat and talked and talked and talked.

Bev Johns called Sharon in the evening. Joan and I had done most of the talking so far. Sharon needed to talk. Bev gave her that opportunity.

Sometimes, people in shock will say, "I don't want to talk about it," I think they're wrong; I'm convinced that retreat and withdrawal during this time can have serious repercussions later.

But I can understand the rationale. We've all been told, as children, "Don't make such a fuss – it's not serious." We fear that this pain tearing us apart may not really be as serious as we think it is. We don't want to be cry-babies.

The opportunity to talk it through reassures us that our loss really is big enough to justify our feelings. Sharing the story, over and over, also allows us to distance ourselves from the event. We get some perspective; the mountain no longer seems so ready to crush us.

This reassurance is especially important for those whose loss is less obvious. A fired executive, for example, probably got a fairly good severance package. She still has her home, her children, her spouse. She has no visible scars. But her self-respect, her sense of worth has been destroyed. She needs to be able to talk about that. Platitudes, assurances that she'll get over it, even suggestions that it may turn out to be a good thing in the long run, all miss the point. What she needs is neither comfort nor encouragement – she needs to know that the overwhelming pain she feels is justified.

A Ceremony of Acknowledgment

Stephen's memorial service was Wednesday evening, four days after his death. It gave us something specific, a real and concrete ritual, to focus on. Those suffering other kinds of grief don't have that opportunity. There are no rituals for the person who has been fired, or laid off, or summarily retired, or who cannot find a job anywhere. Such a person has nothing. No ceremony to acknowledge this new existence. No colleagues to provide support. Nothing to look forward to but days and days of nothing worth doing.

Nor has someone going through separation or divorce any focus for the transition. Counseling sessions, if there were any during the marriage breakdown, provided a kind of regular ritual. But they have ended. Some people even look forward to visits with the lawyer – the meetings at least punctuate an otherwise endless desert of hopelessness.

Nancy Reeves, a psychologist in Victoria, British

Columbia, helps her clients devise rituals for times of crisis and transition. Rituals are part of the healing process, she says. "A ritual provides some structure for that time of transition. Although people don't know how they're going to feel or react, at least they know what they're going to do."

Society has provided rituals for those bereaved by death. Arrangements for the funeral or memorial service can be tackled, can be dealt with. The details may be a straw to grasp at while drowning. But even a straw is better than going under.

Journal entry   August 10

We were dreading the service this evening, but it was okay.

Grant Kerr, in his comments, told of Stephen tying his shoelaces together during a prayer.

I don't remember what Don Johns said; we were too tired, too numb, by this time, to retain anything more.

There were more than 350 people there. They filled both balconies, and there were rows and rows of chairs set up behind the regular pews. The doctor, the nurses from Sick Kids Hospital all came out, even though they had to switch their shifts to make it. Jim and Donna Sinclair drove down from North Bay – a five hour drive – to attend the service.

Mixed Up Priorities

William Sargant claims that in periods of intense stress, our minds lose – and may even reverse – their normal priorities.

Usually, we can distinguish between the importance of, say, eating a wholesome meal and polishing the silver. Under a basic level of stress, says Sargant, all concerns start to rate equal importance. The arrival of the mail matters just as much as evicting a family of squirrels from the basement.

Under higher stress, Sargant continues, people often reverse their normal priorities. Minor items become major; major items become insignificant. We become obsessed with responding to sympathy cards but completely forget about a doctor's appointment.

In this "paradoxical" phase, says Sargant, "the patient receives a greater emotional stimulus... from a small stimulus than a larger one. In this state, people may get intense emotional satisfaction from quite minor happenings, while remaining indifferent to normally overwhelming blows of fortune." It's a defense mechanism, a way of protecting ourselves from those "overwhelming blows." (*Battle for the Mind*, p. 10–11)

For some reason, the day after Stephen's memorial service, the three of us became convinced that we had to, simply had to, express our thanks to the staff of the cystic fibrosis ward at Toronto's Hospital for Sick Children, where Stephen had died. The rain poured down all day. Joan and Sharon got up, looked at the weather, and went back to bed for the rest of the morning. There seemed little reason to get up – let alone go out.

But by the afternoon, we had bought flowers, driven downtown, and gotten soaked walking from the parking garage into the hospital.

It was not rational to take flowers into the place that had the most painful memories of our lives. It was shock.

Journal entry   August 11

The worst moment was pushing open the doors of Ward 7E. We have done it too many times before, always fearing the worst. All the old fears came flooding back. But the warmth from the staff cushioned the pain. We didn't go to his room, though.

What You Can Do

If you're the person in shock, there is nothing you can do. Not until the shock passes, and you begin to feel the other normal emotions of deep grief.

Besides, if you're in shock, you won't recognize it at the time.

If someone you know is going through shock, the best thing you can do is stay close. Don't treat that person's behavior as abnormal; let them talk about anything they want to talk about, whether or not it relates to their trauma. Don't try to make the person cry; don't try to move the grieving process along. If your friend is bright and cheerful, don't try to impose mourning because you think it's more appropriate, and don't wear a long face yourself.

Express your sympathy. Share a story or two about your recollections. Go ahead and cry, if you feel like it. But don't make things any more difficult for the survivors than they already are.

Just keep them company. It doesn't sound like much, but it's crucial. The worst feeling – the feeling the grieving person is struggling against – is the sense of having been abandoned. By the person who died, by a loved one, by colleagues, by God.

Shock, by its very nature, is a short-term reaction. It will pass. What matters is that the grieving person has friends nearby when it does. Because when the shock does pass, that person will be incredibly lonely.

Denial

Aside from the parade of sympathizers, the first few days after Stephen died felt much as if he had simply gone away to camp for the summer. We almost expected to get a phone call from him, asking us to send up his spare bathing suit, or his sunglasses, or whatever else he had forgotten. He almost always forgot something.

We had moved into the state that Elisabeth Kübler-Ross called denial. It's hard to deny that a death had taken place. Or that a factory has closed. Or that a marriage has ended. Or that your son or daughter has been arrested for a crime.

But we all do it.

Consciously, we know exactly what's happened. When you have held a stiffening body in your arms, when you have felt the warmth of life fading away, first from fingers, then from limbs, then from the chest – you know too well that someone has died.

But the head and the heart move at different speeds. Intellectually, you can acknowledge that you're now unemployed. Emotionally, you're still tied to your former life. You'll look for items about that firm in the paper. You'll notice its advertising. You may drop in on former colleagues, just to see what's going on. You'll probably continue to get up at the same time, as if you still had a job to go to.

Something has ended – that's a fact.

But facts rule the head, not the heart. The heart is governed by emotions. The head may know that something had ended, but the heart simply doesn't want to admit it. Yet. One of the early letters I wrote to Stephen recognized, rather inarticulately, that denial.

> October 3
>
> Dear son,
>
> It's funny. My mind and my emotions can accept that you have died, and have gone. I can imagine you not being here, not being around to work on the car or lie on the couch or to share an idea with. But I still cannot imagine, I cannot begin to imagine, me without you.

Some eight years later, Sharon had completed her Master's degree, and had moved to Edmonton to work as an ergonomist – a specialist in the workplace environment. She lost her job in a personality conflict with her supervisor.

"After I got fired from the Workers' Compensation Board," she told me, "I kept expecting them to call me, any day, and tell me that they had decided they had made a mistake, and would I come back again, because they were firing my boss."

Denial Goes Underground

Denial is a sneaky emotion. You think you've accepted reality – then you find that you haven't.

About a week after Stephen's death, our heads convinced us that we had to do something about his bank accounts, his life insurance policy. That meant going through his room, cataloguing his belongings for estate purposes.

> Journal entry   August 15
>
> In the evening we went through Stephen's room, trying to list his assets. There is so little left of him, and we feel we are prying, opening his drawers.
>
> Joan starts crying: "He's not coming back... but I want him to..."
>
> She doesn't want to believe he's gone.

More than three months later, I had to go into Stephen's room again.

December 4

Dear Stephen,

I found it hard going into your room. Suddenly, there was so much to remind me of you all over again. I felt as If I were intruding into your private space.

I almost had to force myself to open the drawer in which we put your private papers. I found again the notes that you had made to yourself about the progress of your illness. You had calculated all the time that you would be tied down, what that left in free time, what the implications were for university courses.

And at the bottom, the question that continues to haunt me, because it reveals that you knew how close you were coming to the end. You wrote in your shaky printing: "I'm worried about the big one coming and taking me."

My reactions, entering Stephen's room, prowling through his papers, showed that I still thought of it as *his* room. *His* papers. *His* territory. I had the same hesitation to walk in as I did when he was a teenager.

Involuntary reactions reveal the denial. For months, Joan kept seeing tall, skinny, tow-headed teenagers when she rode the subway to and from work. Of course she knew it wasn't Stephen. But each time she waited, barely daring to breathe, until the teenager turned around.

> September 18
>
> Dear Stephen,
>
> Kathy [Haney, our next door neighbor] looks out onto the street, and sees a car coming, and thinks, "Oh, there's Stephen." Or she's driving along, and sees someone who looks like you – tall, skinny, blonde, who walks with a little kick to the end of each step – and wants to stop to give you a lift.
>
> Last Friday night, Joan went out food shopping, I was downstairs in the basement, when I heard the back door open and shut. Something inside me wondered if it might be you, if this whole thing had been some kind of a night-mare, and that you really had come back, somehow. I'd probably have to check myself into the loony bin for a spell, if it had been you – but it would have been worth it.

For months, every time someone opened the back door without knocking, I held my breath, half expecting to hear Stephen's voice call "Ullo, 'ullo?"

For months after my mother died, my father still called out. "Hi, dear, I'm home!" when he opened the back door of their home.

Literal denial lasts only a short time. For a few months, a grieving person wails, "It can't be over!" "I don't believe it!"

Emotional denial goes underground. Verbally, you ad-mit that a death has occurred, a job has ended, a marriage has broken up. But for a surprisingly long time, you don't believe it. Somewhere, deep down inside, an undercurrent continues to tell you, "Maybe it's all a mistake. Maybe it didn't really happen."

Letters to a Dead Son

I think I began to deal with my emotional denial when I

started writing letters to Stephen. Writing letters to a dead person is not a particularly rational thing to do. But it was, for me, a very helpful thing.

The letters started almost a month after his death. August 28th was dull; I remember it as rainy. I couldn't go outside and bury my grief in physical activity. Out of boredom, I picked up an English translation of Antoine de Saint-Exupery's classic children's book, *The Little Prince*. I had picked up many books during the previous three weeks; I soon put them all down again. None touched my current experience.

But *The Little Prince* spoke to me as no other book had. It told me my own story – the story of someone who encountered a wonderful, enchanted child, a child who blessed the writer's life with enthusiasm and insight. A child who could only stay a limited time, and then had to go away again. A child whose absence made the world a terribly lonely place.

I read that book, and cried. I must have cried for an hour. I cried as I had not cried since the first days after Stephen's death.

And then, for therapy, I went downstairs and wrote to Stephen about the experience. For I could think of no one else who could appreciate it but my own "Little Prince."

August 28

Dear Stephen,

· While you were struggling for life on the Thursday evening, I assured you that it had all been worthwhile, no matter how much trouble it seemed at the time, and I meant that. A thousand times over, I meant it. Because it was for you.

But we don't have you any more. All we have now is the memory of you, echoing around in the emptiness of our lives.

Today, reading that book of Sharon's, *The Little Prince*, out of the fable and fantasy at last came a glimpse of hope, that somehow you *are*, still, somewhere, somehow.

Perhaps you read it. I hope you did. Particularly at the end, where the little prince from another planet explains about going back to his own planet.

I can't help thinking of you as that little prince. You knew you were going to fade away. You knew that the only release would be through the doorway of death, and that it would look painful. You were frightened by it, but in the end, you knew you would have to welcome it. Like the little prince who told his friend the author not to watch, not to see, you didn't want us to be pained by what was happening, and yet, like him, you were relieved to have us there.

Oh, Stephen, my son, my son, you are my little prince. If only you could come back.

Over the next four months, I wrote to Stephen almost daily. Were the letters themselves a a denial of his death? I don't think so. I see them as the beginnings of acceptance. Of death in general, and of his death in particular.

But that acceptance did not come easily.

September 1

Dear Stephen,

I really need to write to you this morning. Yesterday was a real downer for me.

It was my birthday.

About a week ago, Mum [Joan] asked me what I

> wanted for my birthday. I couldn't answer. The one thing that I wanted most in all the world I couldn't have. I wanted you back with us.
>
> At one time I kept wishing that I could see you just once more healthy, enjoying a game of basketball, ducking past a checker, driving in and floating — as only you could do — floating through the air for a slam-dunk. I wouldn't even ask for that any more — I'd take you as sick as you were in the hospital, just to have you with us again.

One of the more difficult acts, after any death, is clearing out the dead person's clothes. It seems so final. Until then, you can still kid yourself that *if* that person came back – unless you have been through it yourself, you cannot imagine the longing in that "if" – he or she could still use those clothes. To clean out the closets means admitting the person won't come back. Ever.

"It is not an easy task to do away with the belongings of a loved one," comments Harriet Sarnoff Schiff in her book *Living Through Mourning: Finding Comfort and Hope when a Loved One Has Died.* "First of all, you cherish them, right down to the worn pair of slippers you always threatened to throw out. Suddenly instead of being an affront, they have become cherished reminders... Suddenly things take on an entire new aspect: they become dear heirlooms rather than junk, and you want to keep them." (p. 103)

We cleaned out my mother's closet a week after she died. We hoped someone else could benefit from her suits, her coats. But at the same time, we hated the thought of some stranger wearing those precious, those memory-filled, pieces of clothing.

We had the same struggle dealing with Stephen's clothes.

September 12

Dear son,

Yesterday, Joan finally got the courage to move your cloth-ing, the shirts and jeans that we had packed into boxes long ago, down to the front hall so that I can take them over to the Goodwill Industries drop boxes in the plaza.

She couldn't throw out your old striped blue house-coat, though. Sharon said, before she left, that it was too much a part of you. We agreed. When you were in the hospital, on that last night, I wanted to cry on your shoul-der, and couldn't. Because others were at your side at the time. And they had as much right to be there as I did. Your housecoat was hanging on the wall. It was you, and so I cried into it, instead. You probably never knew that...

At few items – a sports jacket, his bright blue windbreaker – would fit me. We kept them. A few others, Sharon wanted to take to university with her.

The rest we gave to Goodwill Industries.

September 12

... This afternoon, I took the boxes to the plaza.

It was hard enough sorting things out. But somehow, as long as they sat in the front hall, waiting for something to be done with them, it was possible to think that they could be salvaged. If – praise God – you were to come striding through the door, they could still be taken back up to your room, could still be used.

When I raised the first box to push it through the trap door, I felt much as I did when I saw the nurse getting ready to inject the morphine into your IV solution. I wanted then to leap across the bed, to knock the syringe from her hand, at the very least to shout out "Stop! Wait! Think what we're doing..." Because once that started, it was an admission that there was no longer any hope, no chance for recovery.

I didn't do it then, because the decision had already been made, in a sense. It's like so much of life – when we come to the time to make a decision, we discover that it has already been made. Each step we make, getting to this moment, has committed us to this decision.

At such times, the only choice is, "Do I affirm what I have previously decided and continue on the same course? Or do I repudiate what I have previously done?"

I once preached on that subject, at the chapel of United Church House. I argued that for Jesus, the die of his crucifixion was cast when he decided to go to Jerusalem, in spite of his disciples' protests. It wasn't when he refused to answer his accusers, nor when he cleared the moneychangers from the temple. But the time when he could have changed things was when he "set his face to go to Jerusalem." From then on, everything was simply an unfolding of the plot.

When you lay there in the hospital, in a sense, the decision had been made earlier, when we agreed that you would have no extraordinary life support systems. No respirator. No surgery. No machines keeping you alive.

Once that decision had been made, we had no choice but to go along with the morphine – or to let you suffer more, which we could not do. We couldn't stand any more suffering ourselves.

It was the same feeling today, when I took the boxes over. I pushed the first one through. As I heard it hit the pile

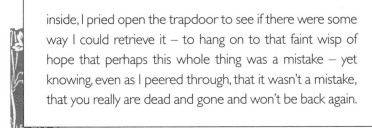

inside, I pried open the trapdoor to see if there were some way I could retrieve it – to hang on to that faint wisp of hope that perhaps this whole thing was a mistake – yet knowing, even as I peered through, that it wasn't a mistake, that you really are dead and gone and won't be back again.

Many times during those first months of mourning, I thought that I had fully accepted Stephen's death. And then something unexpected would make me realize that I hadn't.

Denial persisted for months, I think that writing letters helped me identify that denial, and perhaps to deal with it, more quickly than Joan and Sharon did. My journal for Wednesday, November 16, contains this note: "Joan on a crying jag this evening, feeling that lostness. 'I'll never see him again....' Full reality just penetrating now."

October 21

Dear son,
Yesterday afternoon I was out at Cannington, speaking to a women's group. After it was over I went for coffee with a couple of women who want to write a book.

When we were talking, one of them said, "I simply cannot imagine losing one of my children. I cannot imagine it."

That's what's happened to us, I think. We have lost you, but we cannot yet imagine it.

Sometime that fall, *People* magazine printed a long article, a digest of a book, about another family who also lost a child to cystic fibrosis. I was particularly struck by the recurring parallels with our own experience.

The girl's name was Angela. She was about eight when she died. Like us, her parents refused to accept that she was dying, even though she knew it. I wrote to Stephen about my realization:

> November 1
>
> ...the parents were not able to admit the finality of what was happening, until almost the end. As if to admit the inexorability of death would mean giving up, ceasing to try, as if it would weaken the other person too much to be risked. As if, in fact, we could deny what we knew in our hearts by not saying it.
>
> I knew you were dying, last September. Perhaps I was dumb not to have seen it sooner, but I didn't. Even so, I couldn't admit it to anyone until this summer. Each time you went into hospital, Joan and Sharon and I wept and consoled each other. But we would break away from our tears and our hugs to say, "We're acting as if he were dying." And then we would try not to act that way.

What You Can Do

If you're the grieving person, you'll probably recognize yourself in this chapter.

There is no way you can intentionally overcome your denial. You can't simply tell yourself to smarten up: the person is dead, the job has closed, the relationship has ended...You already know all that.

About all you can do is keep reminding yourself of the facts. Give yourself a routine, like a checklist. Tell yourself that it's over. Tell yourself, and tell yourself again. Learn to say good-bye to the past, whatever it was. At first, you may not believe yourself. It may be pretense, not conviction. And saying it will not, by itself, guarantee any change. But I can guarantee that if you don't say good-bye, over and over again, you will never break free from the prison of denial.

There is nothing wrong with denial. Everyone experiences it. It becomes dangerous only when it becomes a habit, a permanent rejection of reality.

If you're a friend or associate of someone deep in grief, do not support the denial. Find the fine line between sympathy and support. Express sympathy, by all means. Show that you care. Don't contradict someone who is feeling emotional denial, but don't encourage that denial.

If you're not particularly close, you may unintentionally contribute to denial by avoiding the subject that weighs so heavily on the grieving person. In his book, *The Facts of Death*, Michael A. Simpson describes the "horse on the dining table" syndrome. At a dinner party, says Simpson, "a horse is sitting in the middle of the table. But we all talk as if the horse weren't there, for it would embarrass the host if the guests mentioned it at all, and the host doesn't refer to the horse lest it upset the guests. Though it is ignored in conversation, the horse sits there still, in the center of everyone's thoughts all night." (p. 92)

It's better to talk about that "horse" than to ignore it. You may well be feeling some of the same sense of disbelief, the same denial of reality. By all means, share those feelings. But identify them as denial. Admit that your feelings conflict with reality. Say, "I know it's silly, but I still..."

Callous as this advice may sound, do not try to give the grieving person hope. It's the kindest thing you can do. At this stage of grieving, any hope will focus on a resumption of the old life – and that's no longer possible. They have to move on.

Anger

Stephen had been admitted to hospital in June, to receive treatment for a relatively mild lung infection. Joan and I had already booked a holiday in July; I also had an assignment, to report on the World Council of Churches' General Assembly being held in Vancouver.

When Stephen was admitted to hospital, we asked if we should cancel our plans.

"Is he...?" I had asked, unable to ask Stephen's doctor the question.

"Yes," the doctor said, "he is. But not yet."

I asked then about canceling.

"By all means, go," the doctor assured us. "You may need the strength from that period of relaxation."

We telephoned Stephen, long distance, every day. Sharon visited her brother, almost every day.

October 23

Dear Stephen,

Sharon described one of her visits to you at the hospital. She was there when we telephoned for you.

"He managed to sound so cheerful," she told me. "It sounded as if everything was going really well. Then he went back to his room. And as he was getting back up onto the bed, I heard what sounded like a little whimper. That was all it was, just a whimper. And I looked, and his eyes were just filled with tears.

"All I could do was hold him in my arms, and he literally bawled on my shoulder.

"He wanted so much to get out of that hospital and go home."

Sometimes I wish you had leveled with us a little more, son. Sometimes I wish you hadn't protected us so much from what you knew was coming, and yet weren't willing to inflict on us.

Sharon is angry at the hospital. She thinks that if you had come home, you might not have caught that flu bug. You might still be alive.

I sometimes feel that same way. I think that the hospital gave up trying to save you at a certain point. So they didn't require full therapy, which might have kept your lungs clear a little longer. They didn't give you a diuretic soon enough, and so your chest filled up with fluid, and eventually your heart couldn't cope with it.

That letter sounds fairly subdued. I know there was anger there, though I didn't express it much. After all, I had invested 21 years – almost half of my life – in Stephen. Like any father, I had tried to teach him, to shape him, to encourage him.

If half of my accumulated wealth had suddenly been wiped out in a stock market crash, a fire, a law suit, I would have been extremely angry. With plenty of cause, people would have told me. Especially if I had done everything possible to avert that disaster.

In fact, Joan and I *had* done everything possible to avert Stephen's death. Since he was diagnosed with cystic fibrosis at the age of six, we had given up two to three hours of our lives, every day, to provide the therapy that he needed to keep his lungs clear. We had planned our family holidays around his needs, his abilities, his supply of prescription drugs. We had learned how to take elaborate therapy equipment with us on camping trips. We virtually gave up any control over our own lives and careers.

His death made us feel as if we had thrown away half of our lives.

The Universal Emotion

Of all the emotions associated with grief, I suspect that anger may be the most common.

Denial has to end, eventually. The loss of that self-protection creates anger. And that anger is a first step in recovery.

Yet though anger is almost universal, instinctive, even inevitable, it is one of the emotions that people least want to admit. Certainly, I didn't put much of it into my letters to Stephen.

Some people are honest enough to recognize their feelings. Roland Kawano, an Anglican priest of Japanese Hawaiian ancestry, had a fellow priest die unexpectedly. The two of them had been working together on a multicultural ministry project. Romney Mosely, the other priest, was to make a presentation to the General Synod of the Anglican Church of Canada; Roland, a multiculturalism consultant employed by the United Church of Canada, didn't feel it politically appropriate to address the Synod himself.

Then Mosely dropped dead at the altar of St. Michael and All Angels Anglican Church in Toronto.

In Caribbean fashion, Mosely's coffin was open at his funeral. Those who went forward to the altar to offer prayers had to pass the coffin.

Roland Kawano had very mixed feelings. "There were teardrops all over the top of the altar," he said. "And I couldn't pray. I was too mad at the guy for dying and leaving me holding the bag!

"So that's what I told him."

Roland recognized his feelings. Most grieving people refuse to admit that they are angry. For a variety of reasons, they suppress their feelings.

Unfocused Anger

The problem is – who do you get angry at?

That's not a problem if you've been fired, obviously. But who do you get angry at, when you retire? You knew it was coming. Retirement was not a surprise.

I strongly suspect that the riots by young people in Los Angeles, in Washington, and in Toronto, reflect suppressed anger over the raw deal they feel society has handed them.

In Toronto, the riots may have started with racial tension resulting from a police shooting of a black youth. But as they progressed, film and video showed that the rioters were both black and white. Their common characteristic was youth – a generation brought up to believe that they would do better than their parents, finding that prospect more and more unlikely.

Black youth had an additional source of anger. Despite laws against prejudice, they had all experienced landlords who told them that apartments had been taken. Personnel managers who assured them that jobs had been filled.

Broken dreams and shattered expectations induce grief just as physical death does. A protest march against a court's acquittal of a police officer for shooting a black suspect provided an opportunity to release some of that anger. And a mile of Toronto's main street was devastated by looting and vandalism.

Finding an object for your anger is all too easy in a divorce or a separation. Grief over a failed marriage can embitter a relationship that had survived a number of years. Anger can bubble up over events long suppressed. A divorced minister was astonished to learn, during his separation, that his wife still blamed him for two miscarriages that had happened during their first pastoral appointment in a remote northern town with inadequate medical facilities.

But most people don't want to hear about these

grievances. The listener may also be a friend of the spouse – and may be desperately trying to remain neutral in a highly polarized situation. So, on the surface at least, partners in a breakup often bend over backwards to be fair to the other. Or, if they can't restrain their bitterness, they have to keep the outburst short. Both reactions tend to deny the depth of anger being experienced.

What I think of as "stiff upper lip manners" also inhibits expressions of anger. I could call it the "macho myth" except that I think it affects women as much as men. By any name, it's the social convention that one does not bad–mouth one's opponent. Especially if you've been beaten. You don't cry foul. You don't make a fuss.

If you've been fired, this convention forces you to *seem* to be fair to the boss who fired you. You may be burning up with rage inside, but all you can say is, "We came to a mutually agreeable settlement."

In some ways, I still think of my job with *The United Church Observer* as the best job I ever had. I left mostly because of insoluble personal and philosophical differences with its new editor. The Observer had, at that time, the largest circulation of any church magazine in Canada. I was hurt, and I was angry. But as far as I know, I never said so. Not publicly, anyway. In public, I was studiously impartial. I supported the church's decision-making process. I continued to urge congregations to subscribe to the publication, and to support the church's operating funds.

(Still, in a classic example of denial, I expected for almost two years that the United Church of Canada would realize it had made a mistake and ask me to return!)

Admitting anger is perhaps most difficult when someone has died.

Do you direct your anger at the person who died? That's almost self-contradictory – if you're mad at that person, how can you so badly want him or her back again?

At the doctors, the hospital, the medical staff? Granted, there are occasional cases of incompetence. But usually the professional staff did their best. They certainly did better than you could have done by yourself.

At God? Perhaps.

"Yes," says Darryl Auten, a United Church minister whose son Jamie strangled when he got tangled up in the cord of his bedside lamp during the night. "Get angry at God."

A Cultural Taboo

But it's not easy to get angry at God. Agnostics have the dilemma of getting mad at something they're not sure is there – an exercise in frustration, if there ever was one. And if you're a devout Christian, you've probably been brought up to think of God as omniscient and omnipotent, all-knowing and all-powerful. Presumably, everything God does is for the best. How can you be angry with something done for the best?

In the Christian churches, we have rarely felt free to get cursing mad at God. I suspect that Judaism does a better job of allowing people to express their anger at God. The great figures of the Hebrew Scriptures often fought with God. Abraham argued with God over the destruction of Sodom. Jacob wrestled with God (or something representing God) all night by the Jabbok River, and refused to surrender. In the desert, Moses repeatedly challenged God's impatience with the Hebrew people, and persuaded God to continue the covenant relationship. Jonah railed at God for forgiving the wicked city of Nineveh. Jeremiah built a case against God like a lawyer. Job suggested that his own ethics were higher than God's; God, he charged, had denied him justice, but he himself would not stoop to speak wickedness or to utter deceit. In effect, Job told God, "I will never admit that you are in the right. Till I die, I will not deny my integrity. I will maintain my righteousness and be proud of it."

Even David lamented, "My God, my God, why have you forsaken me..." (Psalm 22) Fully one third of the Psalms are laments – the entire book of Lamentations is an outcry against God.

Yet as Southern Baptist professor Samuel Ballentine observed in a continuing education course I attended, "You would be unlikely to attend any of our contemporary churches and hear a lament. We act as if everything to do with God must be nothing but praise and joy." Anger at God is taboo.

If God is as all powerful, all knowing, and loving as our churches proclaim, then surely that God could act to end the suffering – both God's and ours. But God does not. God did not intervene unilaterally to stop the suffering of six million Jews during the Nazi Holocaust. Nor does God wave a magic wand and relieve the suffering of individual grief.

The dilemma leads some people to deny that there is a God at all. Michael Simpson challenges that reasoning:

> *It is easy to say: "There can be no God, if six million can die." But we don't say: "If Mrs. Cohen dies, then there is no God." At what point does the transition occur? Are we saying: "Even though four million die, I'll still believe in you, God. But five million, and you no longer exist"?*
> (The Facts of Death, *p. 60*)

People die, tragedies happen – and God does not prevent them. Some try to explain this dilemma by calling it God's will; for reasons that are beyond our comprehension, God wanted this to happen. This explanation offers neither comfort nor consolation. Others suggest that God is punishing us for something. Yet such an explanation only adds an extra burden of guilt and self-torment during an already trying time.

Rabbi Elie Wiesel's story of Nazi concentration camps has been told and retold: how the guards hanged a child as a warning to the assembled prisoners, and one prisoner, staring up at the still twitching body, cried out, "In this atrocity, where is God." Wiesel replied, "Up there."

Throughout Stephen's final days in hospital, I had a very real sense of God's presence. I felt that God was suffering with us, and with Stephen.

But after Stephen died, it was God's absence that I felt. Even God had left us. And I think that was what I got angry about. The foundations of my faith had been pulled out from under me – the walls of my world came crashing down. All that I had left was the faith that I had once had faith, the faith that I would someday have faith again.

The Inevitable Emotion

The fact is, you will get angry. At someone, somewhere, sometime.

You'll get angry at almost anyone – at doctors, at lawyers, at counselors, at society, at your family and your colleagues, at innocent bystanders. As author Harriet Sarnoff Schiff explains, "You are ready to snap at the slightest thing that goes awry. Unfortunately in this less than perfect world, much does go awry. Bank tellers make mistakes... Suddenly it may be difficult to hold yourself in check when you see trivial mistakes that you would usually ignore. You are so raw inside that nearly everything becomes an issue." (*Living Through Mourning*, p. 165)

During her extended unemployment, our daughter Sharon caught herself raging about other cars on the road: "I got so angry. I thought, 'That car in front of me is in my way!'"

Within reason, anger is healthy. It's a sign of returning life, of breaking free from the prison imposed by another's fate.

Repressed Rage

My letters to Stephen, as I noted earlier, don't indicate much anger. Even in writing a totally private document, I must have felt inhibited.

Yet I must have been angry. In lashing out, I tended to hit innocent victims. When we started our publishing business, Ralph Milton and I chose to operate two offices, one in western Canada, the other in Toronto. Some of my memos about errors committed by staff in the western office were so venomous that Ralph refused to show them to the people involved.

I consider anger the counterpart to the depression that grows later in the grieving process. Anger decreases as depression increases. But the anger will never totally vanish; a thin thread of it will continue to run even through deep depression. Periodically, it will erupt, like a sudden boil of lava from an apparently dormant volcano.

Sharon counsels injured workers. Many of them experience depression as a result of their disabilities. "Anger is always present in the depression," she tells me.

As long as anger erupts unpredictably, you know you have not finished grieving.

What You Can Do

If you're the grieving person, you can do three things.

1. **Admit your anger.** Admit it to yourself, and to others. Admit that you are probably not being fair, or impartial, or objective.

   Don't let anger become a habit. And don't vent it constantly, predictably.

   But do admit that you are angry.

2. **Focus your anger.** Don't simply lash out at the most convenient subject. Your family, your friends, your colleagues at work, are probably having enough difficulties coping

as it is, without making them the victims of your rage.

Similarly, don't express your anger in your driving habits. That can create other innocent victims – perhaps including yourself.

But do try to determine the source or cause of your anger. Once you know who or what you're mad at, you have a better chance of controlling and channeling your anger. If you don't identify the cause, or worse, if you deny your anger entirely, it will certainly surface in damaging ways.

3. **Find appropriate ways to express your anger.** Neither vandalism nor dangerous driving are suitable ways. Nor is writing venomous memos or poison-pen letters.

If you can't express your anger directly to the source or cause, find some safe place to work off your anger. Since it's not a good idea to physically (or verbally) attack a former employer or former spouse, and since you can't attack someone who has already died, you need some kind of substitute.

In the old days, people could work out their frustrations on the woodpile. If you have a woodpile, use it. Split wood for yourself, for your neighbors, for the old-folks home down the road. Pour some of the energy of anger into digging your garden or shoveling your driveway. The summer after Stephen's death, I put some of my left-over anger into riding my bicycle the length of the Don River that meanders through the city. Some paths were paved, some so impassable I had to carry the bike through the water. A friend, staggering through a marriage separation, said: "I threw things out and cleaned the house like it had never been cleaned before!"

"You have to find some way of dealing physically with your anger," says chaplain Jan Kraus. "Walk, swim, exercise, pound pillows..." It doesn't matter what the activity, as long as it burns off some of the furnace burning you up.

If someone you care about is going through anger, the best thing you can do is be patient.

Be patient if you're the butt of the anger. Almost inevitably, some of that anger will get turned against you, simply because you're an accessible target. Do not retaliate.

Be patient when you're expected to listen to anger directed at someone else. You may not want to hear it. You may not agree with it. But be patient.

At the same time, help the person expressing anger understand what's happening. In the early weeks of grief, the tumult of emotions is probably too great for anyone to hear you, if you do offer some insight. But later on, grief becomes more reflective. When people don't seem aware of their anger, help them recognize it. Help them identify what makes them so angry.

Help them especially if the anger gets turned inwards, in the form of irrational guilt.

Guilt

Anger, turned inwards, becomes guilt.

And feelings of guilt may last even longer than feelings of anger. You can't stay angry at others forever; you never have to give up being angry at yourself.

Two little words characterize guilt feelings: "if only…"

"If only I had understood what he meant…"

"If only I had listened to her more closely…"

"If only I had asked the doctor more questions…"

"If only I had quit smoking…"

"If only…"

Any time you hear yourself uttering those words, you're indulging in guilt feelings. I didn't actually write those words in my letters to Stephen, but the meaning was there, all too clearly.

Sins of Omission

We had two general areas of guilt: about his living, and about his dying.

While Stephen was alive, we felt we had committed all the time and energy we could to his care and treatment. After he died, we began to wonder if we had really done enough.

Stephen and I took two reasonably lengthy bicycle hikes together – along with a crew of Scouts – carrying all our tents, food, and cooking gear in saddlebags and carriers. That is, probably, two more than most fathers manage. But a month after he died, I wrote this to him.

September 5

Dear Stephen,

I wish we had done more bike hiking together. We could have enjoyed that, I think. I should have gone with you, that trip you and Pete and Dave took for your Duke of Edinburgh award. Though I suppose I couldn't have, without jeopardizing your qualification. The award specified you had to go alone.

I wish we had taken the time to work on that hybrid bike you were designing, in which one pedaled lying down on one's back. I think it could have worked. But we were always too busy — me with work, you with university.

October 3

My dear son,

Last Thursday was your birthday. Way back when you were a little boy, Joan used to get frustrated with me, because I always seemed to schedule my trips to gather radio interview material to coincide with your birthday.

I was so preoccupied by the possibilities of the interviews I might get that I never thought about such things as birthdays.

I sometimes argued that it didn't matter that much — you wouldn't know the difference between the 29th of September and a few days earlier or later. It was the party that counted, whenever it was.

I realize now I was wrong. It may not have made any difference to you. But it made a difference to me.

Last Thursday, I wanted to take the day off [to revisit some places we had hiked together]. I didn't make it.

Lonnie Atkinson, who chairs the United Church's Youth unit, got sick and wasn't able to go to the meetings where the budget allocations for the next two years are worked out. He got someone else to take his place Wednesday, and asked me if I would go on Thursday.

So I went, of course.

I have a feeling that I let you down again.

Such feelings do not go away easily. Other letters reflected the same sense of having failed Stephen in some way.

September 7

Dear Stephen,

Your first-month anniversary went by without my noticing it. I don't know whether that's good or bad.

It just slipped by.

I realized the day had gone by with a pang of conscience, as if, in some way, I had let you down. "You won't forget me, will you?" you asked on your last day. And it's as if, already, I had started to forget you, as if I were breaking a promise to you.

Sins of Omission and Commission

Our second set of guilt feelings involved Stephen's dying. He had told us that he wanted no extraordinary measures to keep him alive. He did not want to be put onto a respirator, for example. We agreed.

During his last day of life, a doctor explained to us how the fluid building up in Stephen's chest was causing him distress, how the carbon dioxide building up in his blood was affecting his eyesight and his thinking. The doctor rec-ommended administering morphine. It would help Stephen to relax, he said. It would make his breathing easier, less labored. But, he cautioned, it would hasten the end. If we authorized the morphine, we would give up any hope of Stephen recovering.

We did not know what to do. We wanted to ease Steph-en's struggle, but we did not want to give up. We didn't know how much more of this anguish he could stand; we knew we couldn't stand much more.

But Stephen's own wishes were quite clear. Somehow, despite his weakness, he tugged his oxygen mask off his face. After moistening his tongue with a sip of water, he croaked: "Yes! Now!"

So we acquiesced.

September 12

Dear son,

Bob and Gord Haney came over and installed an air con-ditioner in your window while you were in hospital. It didn't make much noise starting up – but it shut off with a bang and a bump that rattled the window. I worried it would disturb your sleep. But then you had become ac-customed to a vast variety of noises going on around you: from the air pump running all night in your mist tent when you were small, to the hissing and bubbling of an oxygen supply running day and night...

What you had to go through – it doesn't seem fair, son, it just doesn't seem fair.

Sometimes I wonder if we were right in saying that we didn't want any extraordinary life-support systems for you. Perhaps the additional indignity of a respirator would have been no more inconvenience for you, and might have pulled you through this one, and we would still have you with us.

But then probably you would have had to go through the process of dying all over again. Even now, I have trouble accepting that your life could not have been extended indefinitely, if only you could have had another chance.

But you never got that chance. Never had the chance to come back to your cool, dry room, to the mural on your wall, to your books and the stuffed toys from childhood that you never got rid of.

Never...

To some extent, I still wonder if we did right in respecting Stephen's wishes. Had he lived just a few years more, he would have been eligible for a lung transplant. With new lungs, who knows what might have been possible.

Those lingering feelings of guilt were captured in a conversation I had with a friend and teaching colleague, Eric McLuhan. Eric, a devout Roman Catholic, is vigorously opposed to abortion.

"Killing an unborn fetus is murdering a child!" he insisted, leaving no room for equivocation.

"I agree," I replied.

He was surprised. "You do? Then that's all there is to it."

"Not quite," I said. "It's not that black-and-white. You have obviously never murdered a child. I have."

And I told Eric about rejecting extraordinary measures to prolong Stephen's life, and about approving the morphine injection that would hasten his death.

"That's not the same thing," Eric spluttered. "You didn't actually kill him; he was going to die anyway..."

"But I don't know that, Eric," I said quietly. "And I will never know that."

Two Kinds of Guilt

As Darryl Auten reminded me, "If we had no attachment, we would not feel any guilt. Out of deep love, we experience guilt."

Guilt is, unfortunately, a two-edged sword. If you remember, it hurts. If you forget, it hurts. An anonymous storyteller described the dilemma to Michael Simpson:

> *I still can't realize fully that it's happened. I keep catching myself doing things as if he were still here. I'm talking to someone, and I find myself thinking, "I must tell Fred about that." I keep waiting for him to arrive home from work, and start to get up each time I think I hear the car. Other times, I really do manage to forget about him for a while – then I feel guilty when I realize I wasn't thinking of him.* (The Facts of Death, *p. 231)*

Irrational anger and irrational guilt are both common symptoms of grief. There's nothing wrong with either of those feelings, provided they don't harm anyone else.

Sometimes it helps to recognize that these feelings are irrational, that they don't have any basis in fact. If you torment yourself because you had a quarrel with a friend the morning before he died in a freak highway accident, in which a bus driver had a heart attack, crossed the median and erased your friend's oncoming car, you are dealing with irrational guilt. Nothing that you could have done could have changed the outcome.

But sometimes guilt is deserved. If I had been the kind of father who neglected my children, I should have felt guilty. If my neglect or abuse had contributed to Stephen's death, I ought to have felt guilty – guilty enough, perhaps, to change my ways.

If a firm fails because its management made poor decisions, those managers should feel guilty. They contributed to the loss of their own jobs, and the jobs of their employees. If an aged parent dies in a house fire, caused by careless cooking in the kitchen, or smoking in bed, or improperly installed wiring, someone should feel guilty. If a child dies because a parent didn't insist she should wear her seat belt, the parent should feel guilty. If marriage partners discover that their prejudices, their needs, their preoccupations, precipitated a divorce, they should feel guilty.

How do you tell the difference between real and irrational guilt? I can't tell you – only you can decide that. If nothing you could have done would have changed the outcome, any guilt feelings you feel are irrational. However, if some change in your behavior could have prevented the tragedy, or even reduced the chances of it happening, then you have a clear incentive for change.

An awareness of your own shortcomings can be a catalyst for change. Guilt can propel you into taking better training, being more careful, quitting smoking or drinking, changing attitudes...

It's a tough way to learn. But if guilt is justified, then you had better learn. Because if you don't, you're likely to make the same mistake all over again, and go through the same suffering and grief and guilt yet another time. And you'll wonder why everything always happens to you.

What You Can Do

If you yourself are grieving, you will almost certainly catch yourself thinking "If only..."

By the time you are aware of such feelings, you're far enough along in the grieving process to have regained some control over your life. You are no longer on automatic pilot.

So when you feel guilt, stop and think. Ask yourself

whether your guilt is justified or unjustified, rational or irrational.

If in fact you could have done something to avert the tragedy, by making more effort, or applying more skill, or perhaps by doing less, then start deliberately and intentionally reshaping your life now. Not later. Not after you're over all this grieving. But now, while your future is still as uncertain as partially chilled Jello.

Watch out for those tendencies that contributed to the tragedy. Do you get too busy? Do you stick your nose into too many things? Do you dominate others? Do you fail to speak up at the right times? Do you break down under stress?

If your tendencies, your characteristics, had any effect on the major tragedy that launched your grief, they will also have an effect on lesser events of daily life. Start amending those character traits now, before they contribute to another tragedy.

On the other hand, if nothing that you did or could have done affected the tragedy, then you can feel assured that your guilt feelings are irrational and unjustified.

That won't end them. Irrational feelings can never be dispelled rationally. But you can at least offer yourself the comfort of knowing that what you are going through will cure itself, in time.

If someone you care about feels burdened by guilt, there is not much you can do about it. If the guilt is irrational, no amount of assurance will ease that person's emotions. Verbal assurance of any kind – even heated argument to prove that person wrong – is a rational counterattack. Irrational symptoms do not yield to reason.

The most important thing a person overcome by guilt needs is to know he or she is not rejected or despised. In a sense, that person has already rejected herself, come to despise himself. As a friend, a colleague, a family member, you need to show by your attitudes, your words, your presence, that you continue to value and respect the grieving person.

If guilt is justified, a refusal to reject that person becomes even more essential. A mother whose negligence killed her baby, a tycoon whose ambition brought a financial empire crashing down, a receptionist who fouled up a crucial message – these people may feel not only loss, but incompetence and failure. They will need support to start repairing the damage to their self-esteem. They will need encouragement.

Sometimes, when they feel like giving up, they may need your anger to get them moving again. But it needs to be anger *for* them, not *against* them.

Irrational guilt may be harder for friends and associates to deal with, simply because it is irrational. It has no basis that you can sympathize with. But irrational guilt will usually cure itself, given enough time.

As a friend, though, you need to be ready to blow the whistle if guilt becomes a habit. When a person starts using guilt as an excuse, or says "I can't – because..." and launches into a story laden with guilt feelings, that person has turned legitimate grief into a crutch.

Do not accept excuses. Knock the crutch away. Say what you see happening. Say it with love and compassion, but say it. At such times, you become the grieving person's reality therapy.

Mood Swings

Some two months or so after Stephen died, life was settling down again.

That is, Joan and I were getting used to having an empty house. We didn't wake up in the middle of the night, our hearts pounding, thinking we heard a cough coming from Stephen's room.

Sharon had moved away from home, to Queens University. We talked to her every week. We had driven twice to see her, and were starting to know the roads to and from Kingston.

I was beginning to think my emotions were under control. Then, one afternoon, as I was working in my basement office, the phone rang.

October 19

Dear Stephen,

Monday afternoon, I got a call from George S. Henry [the school that both Stephen and Sharon graduated from]. The caller wanted to know if she was coming back for their commencement exercises this weekend.

The caller said they needed to know for sure, because she is to get an award of some kind. The caller wouldn't tell me what the award was – it is supposed to be a surprise.

I went from the telephone dancing into the kitchen on tippy-toe, overflowing with pride, and thinking that at long last Sharon was getting some recognition on her own. She was no longer just your little sister, expected to follow in your footsteps, trying to keep up with your marks. And because I was alone in the house, there was no reason why I shouldn't express myself vocally, so I started to laugh with rejoicing: "Oh, ha ha..."

> And in that instant, I found myself not in laughter but in tears. I hadn't cried for several weeks – perhaps it was just time that I did again, my head leaning against the kitchen counters, little drops of salty water dropping into the dirty dishes...

From laughter to tears, in a fraction of a second. The incredible changeability of emotions is a key symptom of grief.

Initially, of course, I wasn't even aware of these abrupt mood switches. I expected the tears. I also expected – from having read Elisabeth Kübler-Ross – the flashes of anger. I had not, however, had any warning about the range of mood swings that grief can precipitate.

The changes are almost instantaneous. Joan was at work, one day, when a radio somewhere on her floor began playing a tune by Zamfir on the pan flute. It reduced her to helpless tears instantly. Not for any particular reason – Stephen had tolerated Zamfir, but much preferred Elton John. But something about the sound of the pan flute triggered an immediate mood swing.

Joan's reaction is not unusual. Most studies of grief refer to problems encountered in the workplace such as tardiness, crying spells, and a lack of concentration. Harriet Sarnoff Schiff, in *Living Through Mourning*, coined a memorable phrase: tears are merely emotion turned liquid.

This is not necessarily a bad thing – especially for men. Joe Tannenbaum, in his book, *Male and Female Realities: Understanding the Opposite Sex*, suggests that men generally have two and only two states of being: physical and intellectual. They are either *doing* something, or *thinking* about it.

But women, according to Tannenbaum, have four typical states: physical, intellectual, emotional, and spiritual.

That is, to men's doing and thinking, they add spirituality and feeling.

Men have emotions, of course. But they tend to express those emotions physically, with their bodies. Or intellectually, through their minds and words. They find reasons for having those feelings. But women, claims Tannenbaum, can have feelings for no reason at all – they just have them, that's all. Men want to know why. They assume there must always be a cause for feelings. Women, however, don't have to have a cause.

If Tannenbaum is right, then perhaps deep grief is the only time that men can share women's experience. Because the feelings that arrive so unexpectedly don't necessarily have an immediate cause, either.

Of course, being male, I tended to look for cause and effect anyway.

September 12

Dear son,

It's cool this morning.

It tells me that autumn is coming, that the leaves will soon be falling off the trees, that the long shadow of winter is falling over this land. I dread it. I dread the lengthening of nights, the lowering of the sun in the skies, the loss of light and life and warmth. There has been too much light and life and warmth go out of my life already.

In hindsight, I know that there was no cause for the feelings I experienced – other than grief itself. In the middle of a writing assignment, I would see not the paper in front of me but a kid in a blue winter jacket, dragging a log as big as himself towards the campfire on a winter Scout camp.

In the middle of a conversation, I would suddenly see,

not the person I was having the conversation with, but a pale green hospital room with a single night light glowing over a bed.

I would find myself transfixed by a pair of bright blue eyes that had long since closed.

The feelings I experienced were not all sorrow. I relived my frustration with Stephen during his later years, when I feared that he just wasn't trying hard enough to conquer his debility. I felt the joy we had shared tobogganing down a slope in the Don Valley ravine. I heard his raucous laughter when the bottom tore out of the plastic bag into which I was dumping the dirty kitty litter, and the smelly mess poured all over my feet...

Occasionally, I found myself wondering about this phenomenon.

November 17

Dear Stephen,

There must be cycles of grief that we are not aware of. After a couple of weeks of feeling relatively confident in this new life we find ourselves launched into, I was really tearful for the last few days.

Last night I learned I wasn't alone in this. Sharon called, and was doing a lot of crying again down at Queen's.

Joan was in tears when she went to bed last night. She said she broke out crying on the bus the other morning, going to work.

She gets so frustrated trying to put on a happy face at work, dealing with people who only want to have their own cares taken care of, and who have no idea what might be affecting her. She knows that she's lacking in patience with people, and she can't help it.

Katherine Fair Donnelly, in her book *Recovering from the Loss of a Parent,* lists a range of feelings that people in grief may experience: numbness, shock, denial, anger, panic, yearning, fear, hopelessness, helplessness, rage, searching, guilt, depression, craziness, disorganization, refocusing, acceptance, recovering... I could add overwhelming melancholy, hyperactivity, argumentativeness, nostalgia, inability to concentrate... "There are many emotional responses," Donnelly comments. "These responses may be erratic, and at times confusing and frightening." (*Loss of a Parent,* p. 21)

Paradoxically, this very chaos of emotions turns out to be a sign of hope.

Dr. Roberta Temes, author of *Living with an Empty Chair,* calls it the second stage of grieving. The first is the shock of death and its temporary denial – a temporary denial that may last many months.

The next phase, according to Dr. Temes, is disorganization. Only when the numbness has passed can we feel the full impact of our loss. It's the gradual acceptance of the irreversibility of the event that precipitates such a range of emotions.

The changeability of moods can be triggered by almost anything – like Zamfir's music. The trigger is not the cause. Banning the pan flute would not have prevented Joan's tears; canceling the high school celebrations would not have resolved mine.

The triggers themselves may be inconsequential, or even irrelevant. The weather certainly has no direct connection to one's loss. Any symbolic association is purely chance. And yet because it happens every day, the weather does often become a trigger.

> November 1
>
> Dear Stephen,
>
> I really don't think that I am ready for it to be November yet. Just yesterday, it seems, we were suffering through the stifling heat of this last summer, the longest and hottest summer in Toronto's history.
>
> And just yesterday, you died in the hospital.
>
> No, it was a little bit more than yesterday. Because I can now write that without immediately breaking down into helpless sobs.

Someone told me that I would not recover until I had grieved through all the seasons. The advice was too optimistic. Serious grief always takes more than one year.

After Old Testament professor Vern Fawcett died, his widow, Ruth Fawcett, said that she was going to take a year to grieve. A few years later, she admitted: "I had no idea what it would be like." By the end of that first year, she was only beginning to come to terms with how different her life was without her husband.

"Most people don't realize how long the mourning process can last," a grief counselor told Katherine Fair Donnelly. "For many it takes up to three years, with the hardest being the first year with birthdays, holidays, and anniversary dates to be passed through." (*Loss of a Parent*, p. 23)

Still, there is some common sense validity to "grieving through all the seasons." If the weather has any capacity to trigger emotions – and we all know that it has – then one has to experience the withering of life in autumn, the frigid sterility of winter, the bursting of new life in spring, and the lush abundance of summer, in relation to one's own loss.

November 3

Dear Stephen,

Today, it snowed, fine grey-white flakes sifting down. I dread winter. Yet in some ways, perhaps, I find myself looking forward to it, to a blanket that can cover up the lingering agony. The grass was green when you died. The sun was hot. As long as I can see the grass and feel some warmth in the sun, I have a sense still of life continuing. Despite the temperature, the shorter days, the loss of the leaves off the trees, the seasons don't seem to have changed that much.

I need to see the seasons changing, decisively, to realize that time has indeed moved on.

I need to have the snow come down, bandaging my wounds in a thick blanket of white, of stillness.

Perhaps I need to experience the chill death of winter before I can come up again in the spring.

One of the hardest things to recognize, I suspect, is that in grief one may sometimes have no feelings. No emotion. Nothing at all.

November 7

Dear Stephen,

A lady from the Bereaved Parents' Association called me this afternoon.

Their assumption is that only a family that has lost a child can understand what another family is going through. So they have therapy groups for mothers, for fathers, for siblings...

Anyway, this woman called me with a voice dripping sympathy. "Oh, Mr. Taylor," she said, "we are so sorry to hear about the death of your son."

I found myself being quite matter-of-fact about it. After all, it was three months ago that you died – during that time, even a father can get used to recognizing that it has happened. I can't go breaking down every time your name is mentioned.

She seemed to feel, however, that I should be still in the depths of despair. Still dripping anguish, she told me that she had lost two daughters, aged 18 and 20, in a car accident. "The oldest would have been 27 today, as a matter of fact," she intoned sepulchrally.

I gathered from her that most parents, when they lose a child, bottle up their feelings. They put on a brave face. They hide the pain that they are living with. And so for months, perhaps years afterwards, when anyone asks about their child's death, they burst into tears.

Or else they refuse to talk about it at all. As if it hadn't happened. At least, not to them.

I realized how fortunate we have been. Not that you died. Of course not. That was, I think, the single greatest tragedy of my life – certainly of yours. But fortunate that we had a caring congregation around us. That we had friends, and associates, who knew instinctively what to do and how to ask the right things at the right time.

I think of Bette Van Vliet and Barb Griffin and Mary McCowan bringing over casseroles, and Doris MacLean and Maiike Russell with their flowers.

I think of Murray and Jackie Shaver, seeing us in church two Sundays after your death, in tears themselves, recognizing the depths of the kind of pain we must be feeling.

And after the first three weeks ended, and the attention faded away, I think about the ministers I have been fortunate enough to be in touch with: Don Johns and Bob Leland and Bruce Misener, who had the guts to ask the probing questions about what was happening inside me these days. About the questions that I'm struggling with. The thin ice I'm skating on.

I was never allowed to escape from the reality of your death. But at the same time, I was never allowed to drown in it either.

I'm glad there are people like that.

November 8

Dear Stephen,

I realized something a little disturbing about yesterday's telephone call, aside from my sense of surprise that I was able to handle sympathy so matter-of-factly.

Unless this woman from the Bereaved Parents' Association was an exceptionally good actor, she really was still feeling some pain about the deaths of her daughters.

When she talked about that, I was able to make some consoling sounds.

But I didn't feel anything.

And that bothers me.

It makes me wonder if I am doing as well as I had thought.

Paradoxically, this unpredictable drying up of emotion is itself an emotion. No one would ever argue that because a desert is barren, it isn't part of the world's physical land-scape. Yet when we encounter emotional barrenness, we treat it as if it were not part of the emotional landscape.

It is not unemotional. Barrenness is simply one more mood swing in grief's bag of tricks.

November 30

Dear Stephen,

Dear God, doesn't the pain ever go away? Is it ever going to be possible to react normally again? I talk to Claire Cote on the phone about her mother's death, and just an inflection in her voice sends me into tears all over again.

Am I ever going to get rid of this lassitude, this weariness, this inability to concentrate and get myself going on things?

The mood swings of grief are as unpredictable as the toss of dice, a child in a sandbox, a bicycle on ice. You never know what's coming next.

Mood swings are not recovery, because they do not last. But they are a sign that recovery is beginning.

What You Can Do

Strange as this may sound, try to celebrate the roller coaster of your mood swings! Most of the moods will be variations of sorrow, although occasionally you may find yourself in almost hysterical laughter. And sometimes all emotions will dry up like a summer puddle.

There may not be much actual celebration in the moods themselves. But if you can, celebrate the fact that you can again have more than one mood. The sky is not always black any more; it has turned into an unpredictable crazy quilt of castles and ice cream cones, of lurking dragons and gloomy dungeons.

Recall the sterile aridity of your emotions in the first days of your loss, and compare them with the mountain ranges of emotions you now experience. When you can see that variety, you will know that you are in fact on the road to new life.

Keeping a journal will help you keep track of these changes. So will writing letters, like mine to Stephen.

Or you can do a simple exercise. Roy V. Nichols, a funeral director and consultant on death education in Chagrin Falls, Ohio, put together a list of words related to grief. He suggests making several copies of this list. Date one copy; then go through the list, circling the words that match your current state of mind.

surges of emotion
bitterness
fear
futility
resentment
disappointment
helplessness
nervousness
yearning
loss of appetite
anxiety
anguish
sadness
disrupted attention span
dejection
disbelief
weight loss or gain

resignation
numbness
sleeplessness
despair
talkativeness
loneliness
hostility
guilt
emptiness
panic
physical illness
forgetfulness
hypochondria
hopelessness
agitation
sorrow
regret

(from *Living Through Mourning,* page 175-6)

Do the exercise again, in a few weeks.

Repeat the process as the weeks go by. After doing this three or more times, compare the results, and see how you and your world are changing. Even moving from "panic" to "despair" is a sign of progress!

If someone you care about is grieving, you may find the unpredictability of mood changes a bit trying. Just when you expect a quiet dinner, he's numb with pain. You plan a business meeting with a supervisor, and her waterworks are overflowing. You go out for a casual cup of coffee, and find the entire cafe staring at the two of you. You offer sympathy, and get chewed out.

Yes, your friend is unpredictable. But isn't that better than predictably glum? Or chronically miserable? Or brittle as splintered glass?

It's a whole new world; your friend needs a new emotional wardrobe to enter it. Rejoice! Your friend is trying on some new emotions to see how they fit.

Wallowing

Every time I thought about Stephen, it hurt.

Logic says that when something hurts, you stop doing it. Avoidance of pain is the whole principle behind much childhood learning. You put your hand on a hot stove; it burns, so you don't do that any more.

Logically, then, if thinking about something hurts, you should stop thinking about that person or that experience. But grief doesn't work that way. The greater the pain, the more you discover that you can't help thinking about it.

August 28

Dear Stephen

You sat in the bed, the frailest shell of the man I had known, gasping for breath. You started to cough, the cough that had been your trademark ever since you were about three years old. But this time, instead of fighting, you took one short quick breath. Then you paused, and gasped once more.

And you were gone.

Just like that.

No final moment of lucidity. No last struggle. "Do not go gentle into that good night," Dylan Thomas wrote, and I wanted to quote it to you during that last year, how many times I wanted to quote it to you as I saw you slipping down without seeming to rebel against your fate. "Do not go gentle into that good night, but rage, rage against the dying of the light..."

But you wouldn't do it. Not even at the end.

It sounds masochistic. Perhaps it is. I only know from my own experience, from the experiences that others have shared with me, that this "wallowing" in pain is a characteristic symptom of grief.

"I must not forget," Henri Nouwen wrote in *In Memoriam* after his mother's death. "I must remember her even if remembering brings with it pain, sorrow, and sadness."

An Indescribable Experience

It makes no sense to dredge up memories of the person, to deliberately think about those things that hurt you. It would make much more sense to try to forget, to set all that behind you.

Nouwen describes going back to his parents' home after his mother's funeral:

I walked into her little study... I sat at her desk and looked at some notes she had written in the days before she went to hospital. Suddenly, I realized that she who had written me every week would never write me again. In a drawer, I found my name written on folders and envelopes, and realized how often she had thought of me as she sat there. Only now did I realize that I had become a different man, a man without a mother... (In Memoriam, p. 49)

We each went over every detail of Stephen's life in our minds. Sometimes we talked about it; sometimes we just thought about it. We recalled the smallest details, the tiniest implications.

> August 28
>
> Dear Stephen,
> When you were a very small boy, and we lived in North Vancouver, I took a picture of you, looking out the front window of that house at the street. It seemed to me that it

captured some of the pathos that I knew would be part of your life. Don't ask me how I knew, I just knew, somehow, that you would be an outsider to the life that most other children led, looking out at it but always somehow shut out of it by a barrier as invisible as the glass in that window.

I was right, you know. CF was a barrier for you. The fact that you had to have therapy, had to have pills, or perhaps especially that you knew that life had a temporariness for you that it didn't for others, set you apart. You were different. I'm sure that in some way you are still different.

Integrating Past and Present

After Stephen died, I thought the newspapers should have published a major obituary on him, to acknowledge his heroic struggle against terminal illness. Of course, they didn't. The obituaries were of people who built financial empires, or served a union for 50 years, or had won political office. Not of a 21-year-old kid who had managed to make life an adventure despite his disabilities.

I thought that if the newspapers weren't going to write his story, I would have to. I bought several packages of 3x5 file cards. Every time I remembered another incident from his life, I made notes of it and filed it carefully in a grey plastic filing box.

Over the next months, that box filled until I couldn't jam another card into it. I cried over every one of those file cards. But I didn't stop doing it.

That's why I call it "wallowing." It's almost as if you enjoyed the pain.

I see a similar symptom among immigrants and refugees. Some come to a new country with high hopes; others have no choice – they have to escape from intolerable conditions. But once into the new country, they don't stop remembering the old life. In a sense, they deliberately evoke memories by associating with others who also share those memories, painful or pleasant. They tell each other stories of how things used to be.

Even painful memories are familiar and comforting in an unfamiliar, utterly strange new setting.

The same phenomenon occurred in the early Christian church, I suspect. It must have been agonizing for those early disciples – both men and women – to recount the stories of the person they had thought of as the Messiah, the long-promised hope. But because they told those stories over and over, to each other, to others, the stories became widely known.

If they had not "wallowed" in the agony of the crucifixion, in the guilt of their failure to understand, the loneliness of their separation from their teacher, we would not have the Christian gospels today.

By wallowing, we try to keep the memories alive – because when the memories die, so does part of our lives.

Learning to Accept the Unacceptable

By wallowing, I believe, we learn to accept the utterly unacceptable. Before we can move on to a new life, we have to assure ourselves that we have a firm grounding in the old life, no matter how painful that remembering may be.

One of the first things we did, as a family, was to revisit the summer camp where Stephen had been working earlier that same summer.

Journal entry   August 13

Drive up to Lake Couchiching and the camp. The road is lined with memories – places we bought pumpkins, or corn, or cut bulrushes, or watched boats in the locks, or went swimming...

In a time of personal pain, even happy events take on bitter-sweet overtones. I remembered clambering with Stephen over a rock bluff at my Aunt Eleanor's cottage, planning ways of building a cottage there – a lack of money never stopped us from dreaming! It had been a delightful afternoon; now it was stained by the knowledge it could never happen again.

Some moments took on a golden glow they didn't have at the time. Repairing a recalcitrant car in the middle of winter, with the thermometer far below freezing, with frigid metal tools sucking warmth out of unprotected fingertips, is no fun. I do such tasks only out of necessity, never for pleasure. But because Stephen and I had worked at such things together, I wished it could happen again.

Like photographs falling out of an old album, memories spill over each other. And you treasure every one, joyful or painful.

September 8

Dear Stephen,

I try to remember the blue skies and fresh breezes of our adventures when we were camping or canoeing, and even as I conjure them up in my mind, another picture is super-imposed on them – of you in that pale-green hospital room.

I see you, too weak to talk, making hand gestures to tell the doctors how you are.

I try to think about your courage in living, refusing to ask for special concessions in school, in hockey, in Scouts. I try to remember how you loaded your pocket up with pills to go to a restaurant so that you could slip them unobtrusively into your mouth with your meal; how you wouldn't let us tell your teachers in high school about CF; how you rose above your limitations to tell that guy who was making a film about handicapped people, "I am not handicapped!"

And what I see instead is you refusing to look for sympathy or pity, even as you explain to Joan that you probably have less than two days left.

I try to think of you walking home from university, your head down against the winter wind, your knapsack on your back, your hiking boots making seven-league strides along the pavement...

And instead I see you lifting the oxygen mask off your face and rinsing your mouth with a sip of water so that your tongue would work a little better, and I hear your voice croaking out: "I'm sorry if I've been a bother to you."

I try to think of you loading up the car to head off to Camp Couchiching, impatient to be away out of the city, out to the trees and the cabins and the lake. I try to remember you listening with a half-grin on your face, tolerating our last minute advice, awkwardly embarrassed that Joan wanted to give you a hug.

And instead I remember the skin clinging to your cheekbones as we wiped the sweat and the moisture from the oxygen mask off your face, gently wiping your eyes, your forehead, your lips, with a tissue.

I remember the feel of your arms going around me to give me a final hug.

And perhaps more indelibly than anything else, I remember the tears forming in the corners of your eyes, tears when you had no more energy left to sob, to talk, to explain, no more energy even to hold your eyes open, but the tears formed under your closed eyelids and seeped slowly out at the corners.

Will I ever forget you? Oh God, dear God, no.

From a literary point of view, profound grief is rather like living in a figure of speech. A figure of speech – a metaphor, a simile – does more than simply compare two unlike things. It fuses two otherwise dissimilar things (or experiences) that have, perhaps, only one aspect in common. In that fusing, that overlapping of images, we learn to see both differently.

Grief does much the same. In one sense, you live in a new world. You no longer have available a familiar person, or job, or ability. But you haven't yet given up the old life, the former existence, in which that person, that job, that ability, was so important. The two sets of circumstances are radically different. A great gulf of loss separates the two. You yourself are the common factor. And you belong simultaneously in both your overlapping lives. The experiences of the present illuminate the past; the experiences of the past color the present.

In that sense, perhaps, wallowing in painful memories is not so much a clinging to what used to be, as a way to glean meaning and significance from the experience, meaning and significance that wasn't apparent at the time.

September 5

Dear Stephen,

So many of my memories are when you were much younger. I try to remember details of more recent events, and I can't. I know that they happened, but the details are fuzzy.

But the things we did – going boating in North Vancouver or Prince Rupert, driving across northern B.C. In the car, your early excitement about going camping – those things I can see as if they were still happening.

I have no trouble at all recalling the catch in my throat,

watching you climb the cliff outside Cliffside Apartments, to get to the road to school, wearing your yellow slicker and hat and enormous gumboots. I so wanted to help you but I knew that you had to do it alone.

Or watching you go off to your cabin your first summer at Camp Couchiching, trailing your towel over your shoulder as you walked away under the arch of tall trees. You couldn't look back at us, or you would have cried, and so would we. Bravely, you carried on to whatever your fate was to be, never realizing that ten summers later, that camp would have become your second home.

Painful Process

Although you're starting on a new life, relics of the old life constantly recall a time that has passed.

August 29

Dear Stephen,

The trouble is, son, that everything I do, everything I see, reminds me of you.

One of the nice things about freelancing for the last two years was being at home, here, while you were around. I realize that now. It also means that everything reminds me of you. I get the mail out of the box in the morning, and remember how you used to get it and sort it for me, and bring a pile down to my desk, and dump it brusquely on the left side. I make myself a cup of coffee, and remember how pissed off you got at me for leaving half-drunk cups of cold tea and coffee all over the house.

I start to work at the computer, and remember how you came downstairs at about this time every morning. You sat on the end of the couch for a while, watching me type. After a while you cleared your throat, and asked: "Got time to do some therapy?"

I mowed the lawn last night. Even that reminded me of you. It took a long time to convince you that lawns should be cut well, not because it made any difference to anyone, but because it was worth doing something right. You got so frustrated when I went out after you had finished and pointed out all the strips that hadn't been properly cut because the grass had been pushed down by the wheels.

Constant Reminders

Even if you want to forget, you can't. You're immersed in reminders. Magazine subscriptions keep coming in. A boating magazine refused to cancel Stephen's subscription after three polite notes. Eventually, we had to scrawl the dreadful word "Deceased" across the cover with a thick-nib felt pen and stuff the thing back in the mailbox. Letters keep arriving from people and organizations who haven't heard.

October 21

Dear son,

A letter came in this week from the CF Young Adults group, inviting you to their November and December meetings. I wrote a note to them, asking them to take your name off the mailing list.

Every one of these mailings that comes in addressed to you is like a stab to the heart. This one particularly so – it reminds us of the way in which that group gave you heart and gave you hope. I remember how there was a new light in your eyes the first night you came home and said that there were some CF patients who were actually in their 30s. It was as if the fog had lifted, and suddenly you could see a whole new horizon out there.

But I also remember how shattered you were each time one of your friends died. You didn't show it much – perhaps you even got used to it – but you were always very quiet when yet another person your age or older died. I'm sure you could see the odds of your survival rearranging themselves before your eyes. As each one went, the odds got worse. Each death was like another nail going into your own coffin.

And now, for those surviving CF adults, you have become another nail in their coffins.

Many of the reminders are internal. No one else knows about them but you. That doesn't make them any easier to take either.

A second letter   October 21
Dear son,
While Joan was away and took her clock radio with her, I moved your old clock radio into our room.

For some reason, every time I went to bed, the clock said 11:17. That same clock sat on your little enameled dresser beside your bed in the hospital. When you took that last breath, it said 11:17.

It's just a time. It's no different from 9:23 or 2:48 or any other time. Am I to be haunted by that particular time for the rest of my life?

I have to get used to it, I have to make it common-place again.

Sometimes, talking with groups, I've suggested that the genius of Jesus was that he didn't choose extraordinary events to have his disciples remember him by – torna-does or earthquakes or tongues of fire from a volcano. Those would be so rare that a long time might pass when no one thought of him at all. Perhaps for so long that when they happened, they would have forgotten who to remember. Instead, he chose the most ordinary thing pos-sible, the breaking of bread and drinking of wine. An ev-eryday meal. Something that happened every day.

His followers could have made it commonplace. They could have forced themselves to submerge their remem-brance in humdrum routine. Fortunately, they didn't.

In later years, the church went the opposite way, of course. It made communion such an elaborate special event that it lost all connection to the daily reality of eating a meal together.

Somewhere in between, the truth must lie.

And somewhere in between – between being stricken every time the clock says 11:17 at night and treating it as just another set of numbers – the truth must lie for me too.

Special events always bring back memories, too. "Dates such as a birthday, or anniversary of death, are especially difficult. So are times like Christmas, Thanksgiving, and other family holidays," explain Donna Hohmann Ewy and Rodger Frank Ewy, in their book *Death of a Dream: Miscarriage, Stillbirth, and Newborn Loss.* (Dutton Signet/Penguin, 1984, p. 83)

October 31

Dear Stephen,

It's Halloween. Up and down the street, they still talk about the night you went out as a garbage can, lifting your lid for people to dump their candies and things in.

It's going to be painful, tonight, to open the door and feed those eager little faces, to think back to how things used to be, and to realize that all that is over for us now.

December 1

Dear Stephen,

The date hits me like a cold shock. Already it is December. This will be our first Christmas without you.

Each Christmas, you and Sharon used to sit on the bed in your room figuring out what sort of ridiculous gimmicks you could fill our stocking with this year. I'll never forget the year that you chose elastic bands. Big ones. Small ones. Thin ones. Fat ones. Every time I stuck my hand down the stocking, it came out tangled up in elastic bands. They were all over the bed, all over the floor, all over me!

"I'm just realizing that I will have to do that by myself this year," Sharon said.

I suspect that we'll all see you in the living room, in

your pajamas and housecoat, long bony legs stretched way out into the middle of the floor, carefully picking the tape off your packages.

You won't be there, but for each of us, you will be there.

The genuinely well-meant inquiries of others also contribute to "wallowing" in the past. Without the inquiries, those same grieving people would feel isolated, cut off, and terribly alone in their sorrow. They would suffer the "horse on the dining room table" syndrome – everyone knows it's there, but no one wants to talk about it.

During her visits with the families of patients, hospital chaplain Jan Kraus often asks, "What was that day (that month, that year) like for you?" Usually, people are grateful she asked. They've felt it was unacceptable to talk about that experience, that feeling, because no one asked about it. But no one asked because they were afraid that asking would upset the grieving person.

Of course it will. To ask about that "horse," the grief that others avoid talking about, always brings back the pain. But the pain is part of the healing.

November 11

Dear Stephen,

Ralph is visiting us. Because he hasn't seen me since that awful morning in Vancouver when I got the phone call to come home at once, that your condition was critical, he wasn't going to be satisfied with casual assurances. He wanted to know the truth.

So when he asked, "How are you feeling?" I knew he

really cared. As I talked, I could feel that lump growing in my throat. My lip started to quiver. And my voice broke.

Ralph came over and put his arm around my shoulders. I must have sounded a bit incoherent. The only words going through my mind, over and over, were "Poor little bugger... poor little bugger..."

I'm sorry. I know that would offend you. You weren't little any more. You were taller than me. But in those final days in the hospital, you seemed so frail and vulnerable and helpless and dependent, that I kept seeing you as the baby that we brought home from the hospital almost 22 years before.

You were such a fragile wee mite, dwarfed by your crib and your room. In that strange place, you lay quietly. You didn't demand attention. You just seemed to accept the strangeness of the situation, to accept whatever it was that was happening to you.

There was that same kind of peace to you, as you were dying, waiting for the last breaths to go out of you. I can't help thinking of you as little.

But you never wanted pity. You refused to let your teachers in high school know about your illness because you didn't want any special treatment, even though you got sent out of class because you couldn't stop coughing. Only one teacher ever bothered to find out why you coughed so much. And you asked him to keep it confidential.

You could have asked for special treatment in the school lunch room, so that you could take that handful of pills you needed with each meal to digest your food. But you didn't. Instead, you put up with the inevitable heckling and harassment from other kids who thought that anyone different from themselves had to be a weirdo, a freak.

And when you went into hospital, you wouldn't even let us phone your best friend. You weren't going to ask for something that might seem to be pity.

In that sense, I felt as if I were betraying all that you had struggled for, by thinking "Poor little bugger." But I couldn't help myself. You tried so hard, for so long.

To live a full and normal life.

When that became impossible, to live a full life.

Eventually, just to live.

Until even that wasn't possible any more.

So yes, it was pity. I can't help it. I'm just so sorry that things had to work out the way they did.

That's why I was crying all over again. There should be happy endings to stories like yours.

The Borderline of Self-pity

Unfortunately, wallowing in memory makes it all too easy to become preoccupied with your own feelings. Some claim that the loss of a child, as happened to us, is the worst grief that anyone can experience. But there are no objective measurements of grief. I know what I went through; I don't know how it compares to the loss of a lifelong spouse, or of a marriage, or of a career. I doubt if it is any worse than having a healthy athletic body suddenly reduced by accident to quadriplegic status.

Each person's grief is unique. But that doesn't make it the only grief. Even in the depths of mourning, none of us is the center of the universe. Others are also grieving.

Wallowing may have been therapeutic for me. But it was even more therapeutic to realize that Sharon and Joan had their own causes for grief, and that their grief might be even deeper than my own.

November 17

Dear Stephen,

Joan was in tears when she went to bed last night. The recurring picture in her mind is you lying in the hospital bed. You had already died – the doctor had checked your heart and it had stopped. And yet every now and then some reflex action in your chest muscles, that had spent so many years struggling to draw air into lungs steadily getting choked off by the chronic congestion, kept involuntarily dragging in a great sobbing gasp.

I realize how self-centered I have been in my own grief. If I was close to you, she was much closer. Your life was always physically separate from my own, but you were once part of her life. She carried you in her body for nine months. Her life was your life. She nursed you, held you, comforted you.

When I came home at night, you raced down the hall and tackled me around the kneecaps. But she was with you all day; she spent more time playing with you, talking with you, teaching you…

It's no wonder that when she came in, she rushed to you and flung her arms around your limp body, crying "Oh, my baby, my baby…"

What You Can Do

If you're the one who's grieving – strange as this advice may seem – enjoy it! This may be the only time in your life that you have full freedom to immerse yourself in your emotions and memories, like soaking in a deep hot tub of feelings.

You need to remember, you must remember, to have a

solid rock of memory on which to build new memories. Of course the memories are painful. But it would be a lot more painful to have no memories. So relish each memory. Roll it around in your brain, look at it from every angle. Get to know it **as a memory**.

Because that's ultimately what you have to do. You have to take something, or someone, that's still very much a part of your life, and change that someone or something into a memory. You have to get accustomed to thinking about the mother who died, the lover who left, the job that ended, as a memory, not as a continuing reality.

Dr. Avery Weisman, a grief specialist, refers to something he calls "middle knowledge." That is, it falls somewhere "between open acknowledgment of reality and utter repudiation of it." That's what you're doing – vacillating between acknowledging and repudiating the cause of your sorrow.

So by all means wallow. But beware of letting it become a habit. Beware of letting it turn into permanent self-pity.

If you become preoccupied with your own loss to the exclusion of what others may be feeling, you may well be sliding into self-pity. In my experience, wallowing is a positive value; it makes you more aware of both your own pain and others' pain. Self-pity is narrowing and exclusive; it focuses only on your own suffering, and shuts out others'.

The test, then, is how you react to others, not how they react to you. If they share a story of their own misfortune with you, and you are tempted to brush it aside as trivial, as lesser than your own grief, you may have tipped over the line into self-pity. The universe has started to revolve around your private misery.

On the other hand, if you can find in their grief – whatever it is – some common cause with your own, then grief is still a positive element for you. If someone you care about seems to be wallowing in grief, be patient. One of the worst things you can say is, "Shouldn't you be over this by now?" As author Katherine Fair Donnelly notes, "Everyone's clock ticks at a different speed." (*Loss of a Parent*, p. 181)

You may have been able to accept the death of an old reality, and move on to a new one. But the "wallower" is still trapped in that old reality. He or she cannot move on until that reality turns into memory. That can only be done by living in those memories, by recognizing them as memories not continuing reality.

Michael A. Simpson offers this advice:

The bereaved often feel that no one can appreciate the depth of their feelings, and truly we cannot share their private suffering. But that is not what we seek or need to do. We can accompany them in their grief, while experiencing our own. Quiet companionship can help more than elaborate diversions... Often you will be most helpful by simply listening. Try not to bring up your own problems and losses. Sometimes one hears visitors swapping gory experiences in some sort of macabre Lowlier-than-Thou contest, like veterans showing off their scars... (The Facts of Death, *p. 242*)

When people start talking about something you think they should have put behind them, don't change the subject, and don't upbraid them. Let them talk. Ask questions. Don't tolerate endless repetition of the same story, the same feeling. Use your questions to redirect their attention to other aspects of their memories.

Assure the tellers that it's okay to have memories. But do speak of them as memories; they refer to what has been. Use the past tense – what was, not what is.

Gradually, you will hear the stories change. Listen for the signs of hope, and encourage them.

Searching

For ten years, Stephen had spent his summers at Camp Couchiching, near Orillia. The camp, owned and operated by Toronto Diocese of the Anglican Church of Canada, was turned over every August to cystic fibrosis children.

Stephen had gone there first as a very junior camper. He loved it. For the first time in his life, he was not an oddity, a freak who had to gulp handfuls of pills with each meal, to inhale medicated vapors three times a day, to have his chest pounded mercilessly so that he could cough up green mucus. He was the same as everyone else.

Over the years, he became a senior camper, a counselor in training, a counselor, and eventually camp staff.

Two days after his memorial service, the three of us – Joan and Sharon and I – drove up to Camp Couchiching. Walt Tose, the camp director, took us to the new obstacle course, designed to develop the campers' upper body strength and coordination.

"He's good at this," Walt explained enthusiastically. He corrected himself: "He *was* good at this. He could get around faster than anyone..." There was a pause. "...before he got so weak."

Sharon and I tried out the obstacle course. We didn't do as well as Stephen. All the time, we looked around, as if we might still see a skinny Tarzan with sun-bleached, straw-blonde hair and a lopsided grin watching us.

That Hopeless Hoping

Searching for the past is a frequent symptom of grief. When two young school friends separate, because one of them must move to Winnipeg, they cling to their former relationship. They promise to write to each other regularly.

And they do. For at least a month.

In the same way, a retired professor maintains an office at his former college, though he no longer has any responsibilities there.

When someone dies, the grief is more traumatic, and less rational. Imagination works overtime.

Dr. A.C. Forrest was my boss at *The United Church Observer* until he died. Every day, he walked past my office door to get to his own office at the end of the hall. About a month after his death, someone walked past my office door, someone whose stride, whose bounce, whose haste seemed to match Al's almost exactly. It wasn't Al, of course. It couldn't be. I knew that. Nevertheless, I came rocketing out the door of my office, wild-eyed and white-faced, hoping beyond hope that it was.

Perhaps this is just part of denial. But that overwhelming desire, even need, to revisit the past somehow is so common that I consider it a symptom of grief on its own.

In her book *Necessary Losses,* Judith Viorst documents some instances of grieving people searching for their lost ones: "Beth looks for her husband by going again and again to all of the places they'd gone together. Jeffrey stands in the closet among the clothes his wife used to wear, smelling her smell." (p. 243)

A surprising number of people claim to have seen the person who died, after the death. Joan's mother, for example, is not given to flights of fancy, let alone hallucinations. In their home, Pop Anderson used to get up first. Often, he went out to his workshop and did two or three hours work before breakfast.

One morning, a few weeks after Pop Anderson died, Mom dragged herself out of the empty bed that the two of them once shared. She thought she heard a sound from the kitchen. She thought she smelled coffee perking.

When she went to the kitchen, Pop was there, making

coffee. "It's all right, Florence," he said. "It's all right."

And she knew that it was all right, after all.

I desperately yearned for some such assurance from Stephen. It didn't happen – at least, not the way it happened for Mom Anderson. But for months, I watched for him. I went to places he used to frequent. I listened for his voice – just in case.

October 3

Dear son,

I really wanted to take last Thursday off, to drive up to the Collingwood/Blue Mountain section of the Bruce Trail and to hike a bit by myself through the birch woods south of the road, after the trail comes up from its crossings and recrossings of the Pretty River. The woods would have been lovely about now. Big white-barked trees, their canopy of leaves above turning yellow and orange, thinning now and falling, lying thick on the ground and crunching beneath the steady tramp of boots... The sunlight would have room to shine through, and sharpen the shadows on the ground...

Perhaps, if there had been time, I would also have gone up the other side of the trail, back up the mountain a bit, past the bridge over the little rushing river, up to the trickle of a stream working its way down the hillside to where we camped that night in the pitch blackness, setting up tents helter skelter on the slopes.

I don't know why I particularly wanted to go back to those places. Perhaps I thought that somehow you would be there, still. That I might have one last chance to see you, hear you, sense your presence.

Did I really expect to see Stephen again, in those woods? Or at Camp Couchiching? At the university? In his old hospital ward?

I don't know. For such a search is not a rational response – it is a desperate yearning that cannot be rationalized or explained. It simply happens. If you have not actually experienced it, you cannot imagine how strong, how overwhelmingly powerful, the desire is to see the missing person again.

My own experience leads me, inevitably, to some skepticism about other accounts of resurrection experiences – of which the most famous, certainly, is the resurrection of Jesus.

I cannot squelch a lingering suspicion that the disciples saw Jesus again after his death because they so desperately wanted to see him again. In the depths of longing, the mind can be very susceptible.

Yet the suspicion is countered by a conviction. Hundreds, perhaps thousands, of people have claimed to see Elvis Presley since his death. They've encountered Elvis in gas stations, in fast food restaurants, in their homes, in their cars, in their outboard motor boats. As Michael Farris pointed out in a humorous article in *Rumors* magazine, there are more documented sightings of Elvis Presley than there are of Jesus.

Yet I know of no one whose life has been totally changed by an encounter with Elvis. People have not gone cheerfully and confidently to torture and death because they thought they once saw Elvis in a supermarket. A sighting of their departed idol did not transform Elvis's followers from ignorant wimps to powerful leaders ready to change the world.

But those changes did apparently happen to the followers of Jesus. So I believe that it really was different from my own wishful thinking.

What You Can Do

If you find yourself retracing old ground, recognize first that you're having a completely normal reaction. "Sometimes," said a friend on reading an early draft of this book, "retracing old ground can be a way to reclaim it – to drag it out of the crypt and back into life."

If you keep visiting friends where you once worked, if you want to return to where you spent your honeymoon, if you feel a need to find out which desk your son or daughter sat in at school, you're not crazy. You're normal.

You only stop being normal when the desire to bring back the past, somehow, anyhow, becomes an obsession. When you dedicate the rest of your life to completing the departed one's work. Or unmasking the incompetents who fired you. Or to making your former spouse's life miserable.

The symptoms of grief change with time. If they don't, they have stopped being grief, and have become pathological mental illness.

Recently, the Canadian Coast Guard had to search the Atlantic ocean for survivors of a ship that sank in a winter storm. For three days, they searched. They found one body. After three days, they called off the search. Conceivably, had they searched longer, they might have found more bodies. But they would also have risked creating more bodies, of having more people die in the search.

So by all means, search. But don't risk your own emotional death by continuing it too long.

If someone you care about seems to be constantly dredging up the past, remind yourself that this is not necessarily a sign of mental illness. Provided it doesn't continue too long, it is merely a symptom of grief.

At first, you will be sympathetic. Even encouraging. Then you may begin to feel impatient, frustrated that the other person is unwilling to give up the past. You're right. But don't worry about it unless it persists.

How long is too long? Probably about twice as long as you think it should be. Almost certainly, the other person was more deeply involved in the vanished relationship than you were.

Offer some gentle encouragement for counseling, if the person you care about is not already getting it. I'm not convinced that counseling will help much in the earliest stages of grief. But during this "middle stage" – oscillating between rejection and acceptance of this new reality – wise and sympathetic counseling can help a person steer a new course in life.

Escape

Six months after Stephen died, we spent the last of his bank account on a vacation for ourselves. We flew to St. Lucia and spent seven glorious days in the Caribbean.

It was escape, pure and simple. We felt that we had been through enough pain and turmoil to earn a break for ourselves. For a week, we lazed on beaches with sand as soft as baby powder. For a week, we strolled under palm trees, visited markets where Creole-speaking farmers piled the tables with mangoes and papayas, explored crumbling naval forts, and took trips into the sulfurous crater of a volcano.

For a week, we almost forgot about Stephen.

Almost.

But on the plane back home, I suddenly dissolved into great heaving, racking sobs. Nearby passengers leaned away, as if I had some kind of contagious disease.

I draw two conclusions from that experience.

1. Getting away can be good for you.
2. You can't run away.

I make a distinction here between a change of scene, and a change of life. The change of scene is a good thing. We took our holiday on impulse. We needed it, and it was good for us. But it would have been very bad if we had chucked everything and gone to the Caribbean to live a brand new life. Like it or not, we had to learn to live with a new reality in our lives, the reality of life without Stephen, a reality for which we were totally unprepared – even though we had known since he was seven that he was terminally ill.

After my mother died, Dad took a trip to Britain, to renew contact with all her relatives there. Several years later, Dad remarried. He didn't do it in a rush, to escape the past. After his second wife, Chris, also died, Dad took another trip, this time to New Zealand. "I felt that both of those trips helped me," he told me later. "They helped me get the loss into perspective."

A different perspective – not an irrevocable change. Deciding to become a vegetarian may be a major lifestyle decision, but it can be undone later; selling the family home can't.

Getting away from the memories

When remembering is painful, it's tempting to think of forgetting as an alternative.

November 30

Dear Stephen,

There are times when I almost wish that with a death, everything that could remind us of the dead person would vanish with them.

That's nonsense, of course. At least a third of my early photos would disappear instantly, for you were in so many of them. Yet I value those pictures for myself, as well as for you. Your winter jacket, which I now wear, would have vanished. And what would happen to the basement, to the walls that you and I worked together at building and insulating and paneling?

We tried to forget – for a while – by going to St. Lucia. Others try to forget by getting away from a place that constantly reminds them of their past.

Just a few months after a friend's mother died, his father sold the family home and got rid of most of its contents. The place had too many memories haunting it. But the memories remained, even in the new location. In fact, by his effort to escape, the father may have increased his own difficulties. Now he grieved not only for the loss of a life partner, but also for the loss of familiar surroundings.

Elisabeth Kübler-Ross, the originator of grief studies, cautions against escapism. "While many families express a wish to move soon after the death of a child, to get into another neighborhood 'that does not remind us' of the tragedy or away from the street corner where the fatal accident occurred, this is not a healthy choice, and too many families have regretted such impulsive moves," she wrote in *On Children and Death*. "To get beyond the pain, one must face and acknowledge it and move through the pain, rather than avoid it." (Macmillan, 1983, p.6)

Stress studies suggest that a major change of location ranks close behind the death of a loved one, a divorce or separation, and an enforced change of employment. A person who attempts to cope with the loss of a spouse by quitting his job, selling everything, buying a sailboat and sailing to Tahiti may experience a temporary high in launching the adventure. But somewhere – probably somewhere in the middle of the Pacific – grief will catch up with that person. And it will be worse than if he had stayed, given himself a chance to grow through his grief, and only then, perhaps, attempted another major change in life.

October 23

Dear Stephen,
I came home from a meeting last night, and had a long, long talk with Sharon.

As I suspected, the excitement of getting ready to go to Queen's University meant that she buried her grief at about the three-week stage. Now that the novelty of university is wearing off, that grief refuses to stay buried.

Everyone faces the temptation to bury grief. It never works. Katherine Fair Donnelly writes: "Some bereaved sons and daughters find the pain of mourning too excruciating to bear, and postpone facing their feelings. They become involved with frantic activities to occupy every hour of every day and night... Months or even years later, a seemingly unimportant loss will set off an inappropriate grief reaction." (*Loss of a Parent,* p. 127)

In one such example, a woman's cat died, six months after her father died. She had, to all outward appearances, been coping remarkably well with her father's death. The cat's death almost destroyed her.

People who keep themselves busy don't conquer grief – they simply defer it.

Withdrawing from the World

There are many kinds of escape. Some people try to drown themselves in alcohol, or in short-term sexual affairs. A man a few doors up the street from us took up auto racing after his wife died – his neighbors suggested he was trying to kill himself.

Some try to bury themselves in their careers. "I threw myself into my work 14 hours a day, scrambling to keep ahead of the depression," said a mother who lost her baby before birth. "I now know that I was only putting it off for another time."

Some simply withdraw. I was at a conference of people who had contracted the Human Immunodeficiency Virus (HIV, the precursor to AIDS) through blood transfusions. A woman was infected by a blood transfusion during a difficult childbirth. She didn't learn she was infected until several years later. She was devastated. "My way of dealing with this," she admitted through tears, "was to go home and close all the doors and shut the drapes and shut the world out."

A young hemophiliac, who got the AIDS virus through the whole blood products that kept him from bleeding to death, confirmed the woman's experience. "I did the same," he said. "I drew all the blinds. But I didn't come out for three years!"

Another form of escape sees people yearning for their own childhood, when life seemed much simpler, much easier to bear. In their dreams and fantasies, they imagine themselves back in younger days, when life did not hurt so much – at least in hindsight. In my own case, some 16 months after Stephen died, I bought a sports car. I had not owned a sports car for 35 years. I suspect I was still trying to escape by reverting to a more carefree period of my life.

Some turn to the church. (Or, perhaps, turn back to the church, trying to recapture a sense of belonging they once knew.) I admit my bias here – I welcome that form of escape, and encourage it.

"Religion has been described by its detractors as the opiate of the masses," comments Harriet Sarnoff Schiff. "Some disparagingly call it a crutch. But what is wrong with a crutch if your leg is broken?... How much more necessary is a crutch when your heart is broken? The difference is that the broken heart is invisible." (*Living Through Mourning*, p. 218)

What You Can Do

If you're going through grief yourself, you'll certainly be tempted to think that a new start will help. The best advice I can give is, wait! Don't leap out of the frying pan into the fire.

Don't make any irrevocable changes. Of course you have to make changes, because your life is different now. But don't do anything you can't undo. Don't sell your house – yet. Don't move in with a new partner – yet. Don't throw out that worn teddy-bear – yet.

In the kind of stress that you are living with, the fewer irrevocable changes you can make, the better. Unless, of course, your situation puts you in some kind of physical danger. If industrial pollutants caused your partner's death, get yourself out of danger. If a lifetime of smoking killed your father, and you finally feel motivated to quit smoking yourself, by all means quit. But don't increase your stress unnecessarily.

At the same time, don't enshrine the past. Keeping a daughter's room exactly as she left it, or turning it into a museum of favorite relics, for example, is a way of escaping *into* the past, not a way of escaping *from* it.

Don't do something rash that you'll regret later. One possible way to avoid that is to covenant with a friend not to take any major step without first discussing it thoroughly. You don't necessarily give the friend a veto power. But you will ensure that you don't act impulsively.

If someone close to you shows signs of trying to escape, you're faced with a dilemma.

On the one hand, you don't want to oppose them. Their primary goal is to escape from stress. Opposition will simply increase that stress.

On the other hand, you don't necessarily want to encourage them. Encouragement may seem like the right course, in the short run. Your friend, your spouse, your lover, will seem to show a new vitality, a new sense of purpose. He or she may get quite excited about buying that sailboat, building that cottage, enrolling in that distant university. Remember, though, that when the excitement dies, that person may have to face renewed grief without you present to help.

You'll need tact and diplomacy if the person talks about escaping to some other city, or country. Don't simply point out all the problems that could result from the move – the person probably feels that his or her present problems are so overwhelming that nothing else could possibly be worse. You might, instead, talk about your own loss if the other person does move. The old saying, "Misery loves company," is usually taken to mean that anyone who is miserable will soon make others miserable. But in a different sense, those who are feeling miserable desperately need company. They feel totally alone, isolated, abandoned. The strongest argument against their moving to a totally new location may be the fear of being even more alone than they feel right now.

Gently, tactfully, try to keep the person from doing anything that can't be undone.

Honoring

Life is so short. When it ends, you wonder if it can really be all over, if a life that was worth so much can simply disappear.

That's an underlying reason for the rage, the involuntary anger, when you discover supermarkets open as usual, garbage collections carrying on as if nothing had happened, the trains still running. Something that matters terribly to you has come to an end – and no one seems to care.

And so, in almost anyone, grows the desire to make people care, to make them realize what a cosmic loss occurred in this particular tragedy. That is most true when a person dies; less so when a career ends; perhaps least so in a divorce or separation. After a death of someone highly valued or loved, the survivors feel something very close to a compulsion to tell that person's story.

August 31

My dear son,

When you were in hospital in March, I approached you about the possibility of telling others what it was like to live with living death. You said then that you had thought, several times, about writing something like that.

You never did, of course. Perhaps it was because you lacked confidence in your abilities, or perhaps at that stage you didn't have the energy to do anything extra.

But what you could have said, what you could have communicated to people, was still worthwhile.

If you can't do it, I'd like to. I can't embarrass you any more by writing about you. It was about the time that you went into Donview Junior High that you got so self-conscious about my writing on CF – you figured that even if the story were disguised, everyone would still recognize you. I honored your wishes, all the way through high school and university. But that's not a problem any more.

Obviously, I can't write it from your point of view.

But perhaps I can tell the story of our family – the things you did, the things you couldn't do, the way you coped with some of your adversities (at least the ones that we knew about), all in the light of your knowledge of the finiteness of your life, even if I don't attempt to put it into your own words.

It is something I would like to do, to honor you. It may be something that I have to do, to be able to get myself back to normal life.

"To honor you." That's the key phrase.

Anyone who has been thrown out of work by a plant closure, or who has gone through a divorce, will hardly want to honor the past by lifting it up in print. But someone who had to retire after a long and illustrious career might – to counter a current feeling of being forgotten. Someone who had to move away from a beloved lifelong home might try to idealize that past.

And almost everyone who has lost someone deeply loved to death feels the need to honor that person. Over the last ten years, I have received dozens of manuscripts about someone who has died. Ostensibly, these manuscripts set out to teach the world something about juvenile diabetes, or cancer, or AIDS. But their real purpose was always to ensure that people did not forget the one who had died.

After her father's death, Katherine Tucker Ward transcribed and edited all her father's writings as a missionary in Angola, and printed them as *A Tucker Treasury*. Barry Morris and Vicki Obedkoff put together a collection of letters, poems, and conversations, with Rita Koerber, a close friend who died of cancer at the age of 37. They called it *The Book of Rita's Living*.

I consider myself enormously privileged to have been allowed to read these manuscripts; I feel that I have been allowed to share at the deepest levels of someone else's emotions.

Of course, I wanted to do the same for Stephen.

September 20

Dear son,

I've never seen the justice – that you should die, while some clod whose ambitions are contained within a carton of beer should live to be 70 – unless, of course, cirrhosis of the liver gets him sooner. You had so much to offer the world: enthusiasm, insight, a quick mind, uncommon maturity, wit, humor, courage... You should at least have been able to live long enough to pass some of that to others.

I can't understand these things; I just have to trust that somewhere behind all the unfairness of it, there is a purpose, that somehow God does indeed know what God is doing.

But slowly it is filtering through to me that you did influence people. You influenced them deeply. And you can continue to do it, but you can't do it through yourself any more. It will have to be through me, and through what I can write about you.

Does that make any sense?

I never did write his story. But in a sense, I have told part of his story in every book I have written since then, in every sermon I have preached and in every talk I have given. Even when I don't specifically refer to his death, his death has influenced my perspective on life.

Tangible Forms of Expression

The desire to honor someone – those who are no longer there to earn that respect for themselves – prompts memorial gifts, too. To ensure that that person is not forgotten, people name a room in a church, or provide a reading stand, or launch a scholarship fund or an award. Every time that room or reading stand is used, every time that award is made, people are reminded of the one who has gone.

After Stephen's death, the congregation of Parkwoods United Church launched a memorial fund. We were not initially in favor – we thought it appeared to be exploiting Stephen's memory to extract money for the church. But our minister, Don Johns, had wiser words for us. "These people are grieving too," he said. "Words aren't enough. They've got to *do* something."

November 6

Dear Stephen,

The cheques continue to come in for the Stephen Taylor Memorial Fund at Parkwoods.

Last Sunday, burly Tom Hazel came down the aisle after the service, his big round face beaming, and announced to me – anything Tom does is an announcement – that the fund was going to go over the top.

You probably wouldn't have wanted a fund at all. But as Don Johns explained to us, the people of Parkwoods need some tangible way of expressing the pain that they are feeling. What right have we got, we who are spending so much of our own time and energy struggling to deal with our own pain, to deny them an opportunity?

The money continues to come in. It's over $3,000 now. There should be enough for a big projection screen for the chancel, and for improved lighting in the chancel too. Your presence will be remembered at Parkwoods.

I'm proud of you, son.

Each year on Stephen's birthday, for ten years, we provided flowers for the church. Others do the same for a parent, a brother, a sister, a friend. The bulletin announces who the flowers were given in memory of; once a year, that gift reminds the long-time members of the congregation of someone who was once part of their lives.

Most of the congregation – and I say this without rancor – could easily go a year without ever thinking about Stephen. That gift in memory draws him back to their attention, at least once.

It's a way of honoring him.

Taking Over Another's Role

Stephen loved camping. A couple of years before his death, he talked me into accompanying him on a hike down the most rugged section of the Bruce Trail in Ontario, from Tobermory at the head of the peninsula along the cliffs facing out on Georgian Bay.

We took a week, packing all our food and clothing on our backs. But a week was the maximum time he could manage without returning to the city for intensive therapy.

He needed three kinds of therapy.

One was pills. He could take those with him, and keep up with his recommended dosages.

Another was inhalation therapy. That required electricity, to operate the air compressors that produced the fine medicated mist he had to breathe. While camping, he couldn't get that kind of therapy at all.

The third was postural drainage. Stephen lay head down on a posture board, tilted at varying angles, while we pounded his ribs like a frenzied drummer in a rock band to jiggle loose the mucus clogging his lungs, so that he could cough it out.

We did a bit of postural drainage during our week-long hike down the Bruce Trail. At each campsite, we found a rock or a log that Stephen could drape himself over, while I whumped his chest with my cupped hands. But it didn't work very well. We couldn't get the angle of repose right – and rocks are anything but comfortable to lie on.

Stephen wanted to develop a lightweight, collapsible, posture board that he could carry in his pack. He worked on it during his final months, whenever he had the energy. It would use aluminum tubing, with nylon webbing to lie on.

I found it in his room, a week or so after his death. Incomplete, unfinished.

Often, in grief, survivors feel they must, somehow, carry on the commitments of the dead person. So they take up bird watching, even though they had formerly hated tramping through soggy fields in search of elusive sparrows. Or a recluse tries to continue the other partner's practice of lavish entertaining. Or someone who feels like throwing up at the sight – and certainly the feel – of a worm becomes an avid gardener. Sometimes these new avocations turn into rewarding hobbies and warm new relationships. More often, they become a chore, maintained only out of a sense of obligation to a departed past.

I tried to complete Stephen's work on that portable posture board. For about two months, in my spare time, I struggled with the complications of making it both light enough and strong enough, adjustable enough and comfortable enough.

Idealizing the Past

I tried. And I failed.

It was a double disappointment. I failed in the task itself. And I felt that I had failed Stephen by failing the task. He wouldn't have failed, I was convinced.

Judith Viorst calls this process "canonizing – idealizing – the dead." We turn them into saints, she says. "We feel guilt about our negative feelings... And what we may do to defend against, or alleviate, our guilt is to loudly insist that the person who died was perfect. Idealization... allows us to keep our thoughts pure and to keep guilt at bay. It is also a way of repaying the dead, of making restitution, for all the bad we have done – or imagined we've done – to them." (*Necessary Losses,* p. 242)

She gives examples:

Through identification we can take into ourself aspects of those we have loved and who are now dead – aspects that are often abstract but are on occasion startlingly concrete.

Therapist Lily Pincus describes one woman who took up gardening after her brother, a passionate gardener, had died, and another rather dull woman who acquired a gift for repartee after her husband, the witty one, had died... By taking in the dead – by making them part of what we think, feel, love, want, do – we can both keep them with us and let them go. (Necessary Losses, *p. 249)*

The effort can become a prison, not a release. I was told, very secondhand, of one woman who "canonized" her deceased cousin. In assuming the idealized characteristics of the cousin, the woman slowly changed from a delightful eccentric who brightened every room she entered to a holier-than-thou plaster figure on a pedestal.

October 23

Last night, Sharon and I talked about what we had to learn from you. About how, when someone you love dies, you feel that you need to assume some of their functions, their responsibilities, their personality, even. When my mother died, I felt that I needed to start writing letters to the Irish relatives in her place.

I couldn't, of course. That's the point. We can't ever be someone else. Sharon had a feeling she should be here, to be the son who isn't around anymore, to work with me on the cars, and so on. But that's not possible either.

Books on grief are full of heartwarming stories of husbands who discovered in the tulips that came up the following spring a kind of resurrection of their wives. Or a widow finds her husband's cameras lying around, takes up his hobby of photography and discovers beauty; a child starts attending a parent's synagogue and finds community; a sister steps into an organization's presidency, vacated by her brother's sudden death, and guides it to success in memoriam.

Judith Viorst calls this "identifying." She writes: "We often identify to deal with loss, preserving within ourself – by acquiring, say, the style of dress, the accent, the mannerisms – of someone we must leave or someone who dies." (*Necessary Losses*, p. 53)

Forgive me if I sound cynical. But I don't think any of us can become another person. I was not capable of completing Stephen's attempt to design a posture board that could be carried in a backpack. If I had died instead of him, he could not have taken over my writing abilities. If you're not already in the habit of writing regular letters, or keeping track of birthdays and anniversaries, or of making small talk with strangers, a death is not going to magically change you.

Resurrection of the Living

But if attempts to become another person – to substitute for them, so to speak – are doomed to failure, it is not impossible for us to change ourselves. Death, loss, tragedy – these things often force us to see ourselves in new ways. And if we find ourselves lacking, we can begin to build new habits, and new lives.

I cannot instantly become a brain surgeon or a quantum physicist. But I can identify some of my own undeveloped skills, and start to develop them. You probably will not become a fanatic about African violets or Italian sports cars, but you may become more tolerant of those who are.

In other words, you should not attempt to resurrect the dead person in your body; you should seek your own resurrection.

You will most honor the dead by becoming more like what they wanted you to be – not by becoming like them. They loved you for what you were, and are. By developing the characteristics they valued in you, you honor their memory. Put another way, if you try to become something radically different, you dishonor their love.

If someone loved you for your tolerance, your sense of humor, your generosity, then enhance those traits. If that same person wished you wouldn't leave your socks in the middle of the bedroom floor, learn to pick up after yourself.

A better person is a living memorial. There could be no finer tribute to someone you loved.

What You Can Do

If you're currently convinced that you must assume someone else's role, to ensure that their efforts do not go to waste, nothing I can say in this book will change your mind. Anything that I write – by the nature of language – has to be rationally presented on the page; on this particular compulsion, you are not at present rational.

But you may, someday, feel a deep disappointment that you were unable to achieve your lofty goals. You may feel that you let down someone you loved. Be reassured. You didn't fail. You didn't let anyone down. You tried – that's all that matters. You tried, because you cared.

Instead of thinking about failure, ask yourself how you are different for having made the effort. What have you learned about yourself? How have you grown? How have your attitudes changed?

You may want to do something unusual, something special, to honor the memory of a former life. By all means go ahead and gather up the stories about that person. Write a biography. Make a gift.

But – and this is a terribly hard thing to say – realize that you do it for yourself, not for anyone else.

Do not expect others to feel as strongly as you do. Almost certainly, you will be disappointed. Others may never have met the person you loved, let alone learned to love him or her.

Perhaps most important, do not let loyalty imprison you in the past.

If you see someone you love trying to assume someone else's role, the kindest thing you can do is to be brutally honest. Don't offer encouragement. Offer sympathy, yes – but not encouragement. The one who died loved the survivor for what the survivor was, and is. The survivor will best honor that love by continuing to develop the characteristics which the dead person had valued.

You too may want to honor the dead person, to do something to show how much this person mattered to you. If so, make a memorial gift. But beware of long-term continuing or indefinite commitments. An annual pledge to someone's scholarship fund may not seem like much to commit right now. But if that generosity becomes a burden some day, any attempt to withdraw from your commitment will hurt your friend. Again.

Fatigue

September 10

My dear Stephen,

I am so tired tonight, so tired that I have trouble seeing the letters as I type them, and my fingers simply do not want to cooperate in hitting the keys. Part of that, I know, is driving back from Kingston, and part from not getting a good night's sleep last night. But a lot of it is emotional weariness too.

Yes, we took Sharon down to Queen's University yesterday. So tonight I'm writing to you, the two of us feeling very lonely and adrift in a house that just a few months ago rang with the life and laughter of two children.

It seems awfully quiet.

An inevitable characteristic of grief is weariness – what my mother used to call "bone-weary." That's the kind of fatigue that goes beyond aches and pains, or even tiredness; it gets right into your bones themselves until you can hardly stand up.

Any serious trauma can produce this effect. Major surgery, for example, removes the organ that caused physical debility. But the surgery itself – the physical invasion of the body – creates its own lassitude for weeks afterward, even while healing happens.

Seven years after her brother died, Sharon was living in Edmonton, working as an ergonomist. She became more and more convinced that her supervisor would terminate her new job when her probation period ended. She found herself overwhelmed with weariness.

"I actually went to my doctor," she told me later, "because I thought that there must be something physically wrong with me. I was just so tired, I couldn't get out of the car."

And this weariness can last what seems like forever. And even when you seem to be over it, it can recur.

It must have been about a year after Stephen died that I found myself falling asleep in the afternoons. Falling asleep at work was a little easier for me than for most people, because I still had an office at home. My office had been, in fact, our family room; it still contained the chesterfield that we all once sat on to watch television in the evenings.

I could not concentrate on the manuscript in front of me. The pages blurred; my eyes crossed; my head dropped. The need for a nap was so overpowering that I literally fell over on the chesterfield. At my desk, I simply could not keep my eyes open.

I began to wonder if I had something terribly wrong with me. Perhaps cancer. Or sleeping sickness. Or narcolepsy – I had no idea what narcolepsy was, but it had been a recent disease-of-the-month in *Reader's Digest*.

So I went to see my doctor. Fortunately, I had a wise and perceptive doctor, who understood how long grief can last.

"How long has it been since Stephen died?" he asked, after checking me over.

I told him.

He put my file away. "You can't expect to be recovered yet," he informed me. "This is just your body catching up to the strain it has been through."

"But..." I protested.

He held up his hand to stop me. "After you broke the bone in your foot, how long before you felt you could run and jump the way you could before the injury?"

I had been a decade younger then. But it still took about four months before my foot felt normal again.

"If you had major surgery, you'd expect several months of recuperation," he went on. "You've had more than major surgery. You haven't just lost an organ – you've lost a whole person. It's going to take time."

Longer than You Expect

I had experienced weariness several times while grieving for Stephen. I had no idea how long it could last, or how often it could recur.

> Journal entry   August 12
> Everyone sleeps late. I'm realizing how emotionally draining grief is, and how that exhausts one physically.

In that utter weariness, matters that otherwise could be dealt with easily seem like insuperable burdens.

> Journal entry   August 16
> Near tears all morning. By chance, Joan's clock-radio turned to a U.S. station this morning. Suddenly realized that in all his life, Stephen was never out of Canada. There was so much he wanted to do, so much he could have enjoyed and appreciated.
>   The tears were not helped by paperwork associated with his death: making calls to governments about his driver's licence, to banks, to insurance companies.

> Journal entry   August 19
> Can't find Stephen's bankbooks. When I go over to the bank, they say Stephen's accounts need to be probated, have to

have the courts appoint an executor, etc. And they will need a death certificate before they can do anything.

Called the university about canceling his student registration. They say to send a letter and a death certificate.

I call Hospital for Sick Children about death certificate. They say they don't issue such things. The insurance companies will provide forms for us to sign, to release the information.

At a time like this, we don't need this kind of hassle, this run-around. I break down into tears of frustration just as I did when I was a child, an impotent reaction to injustice.

One evening, after a difficult day, I cracked my head on an open cupboard door. It was too much – I collapsed to the floor and sat there, crying inconsolably.

A friend told us about taking her little dog for a walk, after her husband had died. She had thought she was coping relatively well. But that night, it was raining. She tried to put up her umbrella, and it broke. She ended up on the floor by the front door, weeping, while her little dog licked away the tears running down her cheeks.

Journal entry   August 26
I feel so helpless.

The Delusion of Being in Control

A feeling of helplessness goes with the feeling of weariness. You're being bounced down the rushing river of life, with no more control over what will happen to you than a piece of driftwood has. And you have no energy left to try to influence your course.

One of the more devastating effects of grief is the feeling that you are no longer in control. And in fact, you aren't. You can't control death; you can't control the economy; you can't control another person's emotions.

"Despite all your efforts – efforts that in other areas of your life have rewarded you with financial stability and with prestige – here you have to face something over which you have no control," says Harriet Sarnoff Schiff. (*Living Through Mourning*, p. 186)

Helplessness may invoke aspects of Elisabeth Kübler-Ross's "bargaining" phase of grief. Bargaining, suggest Donna Hohmann Ewy and Rodger Frank Ewy, is "a desperate move to retain some control over a life that has gone out of control." They describe it as "a return to childhood, when we believed we could strike a deal with God." (*Death of a Dream*, p. 77)

Other books talk about deliberately taking control of your life in small steps, thus reducing your sense of powerlessness.

From my own experience, I wonder if that's genuinely possible. Not yet anyway. I suspect that if you try to take control of your life in the depths of grief, you will almost always try it before you're ready. You will take too drastic a step, too soon.

I believe there is some benefit at this time in learning to be helpless, to let others set your agenda, simply to be carried along. It's certainly an exercise in humility. When you go into an insurance office, seeking forms, you are clearly not in charge. Every clerk knows more about what you have to do than you do. And you might as well accept that.

Death of any kind, in fact, is a salutary reminder of our basic powerlessness. Medically, we can delay death. We can even keep bodies alive long after they want to be allowed to die. Emotionally, we can, as the poet Dylan Thomas put it, "rage against the dying of the light." Spiritually, we can assert that death is not the end.

But nothing we can do can triumph over death. Death will come, must come, inevitably, for every one of us. And once it has come, nothing we can do will change it. Our newspapers, our television screens, show us pictures of people wailing over their dead in Iraq, in Bosnia, in Central America. If intensity of emotion could restore anyone to life, those victims would surely recover. But they don't.

Death mocks our pretensions of power. It's worth being reminded of that.

That's physical death I refer to, of course. But much the same holds true for any of the other "deaths" that people grieve: death of a concept, a cause, a job, a marriage. Once it's over, it's over.

In those situations, we like to think we can still do something. We launch an unjust-dismissal lawsuit; we take marital counseling; we make serious efforts to reform our lives. In fact, these actions rarely change anything. If the marriage is genuinely dead, counseling cannot restore the love that once made it work. Winning a wrongful-dismissal suit may achieve vengeance, but it will never restore lost relationships. You won't want to return to your old job anyway – the loyalty had died. Quitting smoking may improve your chances of survival, but it won't undo a tumor that's already growing.

We can neither control nor undo the many deaths in our lives. Power and control is, ultimately, a delusion.

The alternative, however, is equally unpalatable. That is, to opt out of life entirely, to draw the drapes and never face the world again. To quit trying. To give up. That course, no matter how tempting, is a second death. Having lost part of yourself involuntarily, you now voluntarily let the rest of you die too.

No – you now *choose* to let the rest of you die. Because opting out is a decision, a deliberate choice to make no more choices, no more decisions. But if you can make such a far-reaching decision, why can you not also make other decisions?

In fact, you do. Every day, you will make many small decisions. Some have consequences for the future; some don't.

Journal entry   August 26

Spent the evening in the basement. First time it has been cleaned up in three weeks. Then did the main floor. We decided to leave the upstairs for another day…

Journal entry   August 28

Listless this afternoon.

We decided to barbecue salmon steaks for supper.

Insignificant as these decisions appear, they are decisions, nonetheless. And each one asserts that you are not as helpless as you were before.

Physical Symptoms Too

The weariness of grief is not entirely emotional. It has its own physical effects. For example, when I get too little sleep, I tend to develop a sty in my eyelid.

During the weeks after Stephen's death, I got plenty of sleep. Sometimes it seemed that I slept almost constantly. But clearly, even that wasn't enough.

                                        August 29

Dear Stephen,

I am so tired these days. Now, when it is too late, I can begin to appreciate what you must have felt like in the latter days of your illness.

My emotional stress is taking a physical toll. We commonly think of body and spirit as two separate things. But when the spirit is troubled, it takes it out on the body. When the body is weak, it takes it out on the spirit. I marvel, now, that you were able to maintain what activity you did, and keep your spirits as cheerful as they were. Because you were suffering from a weakened body at the same time as you must have been experiencing some intolerable stress, knowing you were dying by degrees, knowing that your hopes and dreams were going to come to naught and in the end all be canceled by death.

How did you do it? How were you able to do it?

I couldn't get out of bed this morning. When I get too tired for my own good, I usually get a sty in my eye. Even though I have been getting lots of sleep, I got one last Friday. I couldn't open the eye when Joan got up at 6:30. I didn't want to open the other eye and start the day. So I pulled up the covers and slept for another three hours.

The physical drain of emotional pain also showed up as a series of colds and flu.

October 5

Dear son,

Yesterday morning, I came down simultaneously with some kind of intestinal flu and a cold. By the time I went to bed, my head felt about as shapeless as a blob of bread dough rising. Joan knew what the night would be like, so she went into your room to sleep. She was sure she wouldn't get much sleep beside me. She was right. About every 15 minutes, I woke, grabbed a tissue, honked, tossed the soggy mess over the side of the bed so that I wouldn't lie on it, and flopped back to slumber, sort of.

The next morning, when I looked at the floor, I thought if must have snowed overnight.

Perhaps at the time I was a little delirious with fever or something. But last night as I lay in bed, sweating, struggling to breathe through my overflowing sinuses, I felt a very close identification with you. It even occurred to me that this could turn into pneumonia, and be serious. People can die of pneumonia. I could die. It would be much like the way you died, with lung congestion eventually just taking over.

And the funny thing was that the prospect didn't frighten me. I knew that if I were going to die, I would fight against it. But somehow I also felt that if dying meant joining you, it couldn't be such a bad thing after all.

Physical effects may continue long after you thought they should be over. Your energy seems to have returned, you have some vigor for living, and still you get sick.

Journal entry   October 25
I'm getting another cold. Sleep two hours in the morning. Go back to bed in the afternoon.

Third cold since Stephen died.

Journal entry   November 24
Still very tired. Fall asleep on chesterfield until 9:30. I cannot get up and move at all — just weary, weary, weary...

Joan and Sharon both expressed some of their tension by clenching their jaws tight while they slept. Joan's jaws were sore for almost a year. Sharon ended up with a distorted bite that required her to wear a "bite plate" at night to correct the way her teeth meshed, for nearly five years.

Studies suggested that severe stress often produces a physical effect. Those who experience two or more major stress-causing events, or one major event and a number of smaller ones, are very likely to come down with some kind of serious illness within the next three years.

In other words, stress has a cumulative effect. The human body may take up to three years, perhaps more, to work through the strain of any major "death" in your life.

There may be no apparent cause and effect. That is, you cannot directly attribute the allergies or the heart attack, the cancer or the colds, to your grief. But they are related, somehow. Sharon, for example, broke her arm part way through her first university year. It was a freak accident. She was helping a classmate close up a trampoline. One wing of the trampoline, pulled shut by springs strong enough to bounce humans high into the air, came slamming down on her wrist. The trampoline had absolutely no connection with Stephen's death. Yet it is, I am sure, no coincidence that her only serious physical injury in some 20 years happened six months after her only brother died.

In the same period, she had pneumonia, the only time in her life.

November 30

Dear Stephen,

Sharon said that she found it almost impossible to apply herself to studies at Queen's. Every time she sat down at her desk, she started crying.

> Joan asked where her picture of you was.
>
> On her desk, Sharon replied.
>
> "Move it," Joan told her. "You don't have to get rid of it. Just get it off your desk and put it where you'll see it only when you want to see it."

Indirectly, Sharon's experience identifies another cause of intense weariness. Perhaps because her friends knew of her own grief, they came to her with theirs. They recognized in Sharon someone who could understand the depth of their own suffering. And though that's understandable, even worth celebrating, it hardly seems fair.

Just when you're barely coping with your own grief, you're expected to help someone else with theirs. I had already experienced that problem, four years before. For months after Al Forrest's death, people called and asked for him on the telephone. Or they encountered me at a meeting and asked, "How is Al these days?" I had to tell them he was dead. The immediacy of their shock meant that they looked to me for support and comfort, when I had few reserves from which to give anything.

When you've got nothing left yourself, it's hard to pay attention to anyone else's pain. My letters to Stephen deal mainly with my own grief; I had no energy for anyone else's pain. Only occasionally did I reflect on what anyone else might be feeling.

> October 21
>
> Dear son,
>
> We're very self-centered, we who have survived. All that I seem to write about is how we are feeling, how difficult we find it to adjust.

> But how are you feeling? How difficult is it for you to adjust?
>
> Ernie Howse pointed out in his book that the survivors lose one person whom they loved from their lives, but the one who dies loses everything.
>
> Death must be a terribly traumatic transition for the one who dies. How are things going for you?

Children particularly tend to get ignored during times of intense grief. "They don't feel it as much as we do," adults think. "They recover more quickly." But we don't know that – we only assume it, because children are less articulate about expressing their grief.

The younger the child, the more likely parents are to brush off the child's grief. When an unborn child dies in a miscarriage, for example, parents will probably assume that their two-year-old can't understand what has happened. The parents are traumatized, note Donna Hohmann Ewy and Rodger Frank Ewy; quite possibly "neither parent has the energy or endurance to pick up the pieces and go on with life, let alone be responsible for someone else's life." (*Death of a Dream*, p. 70)

Fortunately for us, Sharon was an adult. She was able to discuss her feelings with us, and with her friends. And, when she felt she needed more professional help, she had the common sense and courage to go to the Queen's University chaplain.

The weariness, the fatigue, is all too understandable. Ignoring it, however, may have lasting effects.

What You Can Do

If you're feeling overwhelmed by weariness, first of all, make sure that there is no other physical cause for your weariness. Perhaps, with all the rest that's going on, you're just not eating adequate meals. Better nutrition, or vitamin supplements, might make a difference. On the other hand, the weariness you attribute to grief could result from something more serious. Check with your doctor, and be sure.

If there is no other physical cause, then the best advice I can give you is to give in to your weariness. Don't try to deny it; don't try to fight it. Don't try to overcome your fatigue with additional exertion. Do what you have to do, and don't try anything more. Sleep just as much as your body tells you you need to sleep. Even take naps at the office, if you can.

A variety of psychological studies have found that when stress becomes overwhelming, our minds go into a kind of catatonic state. We become walking zombies. During wartime, people in this state sometimes perform superhuman feats of valor and bravery – not intentionally, but often as if it had nothing to do with them at all. Others become paralyzed, babbling idiots, huddled in fetal positions in the bottoms of trenches or shell holes, unable to move.

The total weariness you experience in surviving a death in your life is like a borderline catatonic collapse. You haven't broken down – yet. But your mind and body know that they are approaching their limits. And they start demanding the only cure that works, in war or in grief – rest.

The feeling of weariness will pass. But it will take time.

If someone you know, or live with, or work with, is experiencing this extreme weariness, be patient. (I say that often, but it's good advice.) You won't cure depression by criticism or scorn. You may incite enough anger to spur the person temporarily out of lassitude, but you may also risk your relationship with that person.

Most grieving people have enough of an ingrained work ethic to do all the specific tasks required of him or her, though not necessarily according to prescribed schedules.

But you should not expect the person to make crucial decisions during this period of grief. An executive who cannot hold up her head from shear weariness will find it almost impossible to focus her thoughts on million-dollar decisions. If a man feels powerless and helpless, he is not in the best state to make decisions that determine the lives of others.

Do not expect people overcome by the weariness of grief to do anything that you would not expect of a person recovering from a mental breakdown. Treat them normally – but without unrealistic expectations.

Apathy

Sometime during the autumn after Stephen died, we realized that we didn't have enough money to send Sharon to university. The trouble was, she was already there. We had paid her tuition. We had paid the beginning of her residence fees. Now we were learning how much her books cost, and her gym fees, and her association fees.

At any other time, I would have fretted myself into a frenzy, trying to figure out a way around our financial impasse. But in the depths of grief, it simply didn't matter. If the worst came to the worst, I figured, we'd sell our car. Or our house. Or something.

I wasn't being brave, or optimistic, or anything like that. I simply didn't care. I didn't have the energy to care.

Part of the apathy results from the weariness I described in the previous chapter. But an even bigger part came from the sense that there was no future. I had nothing left to live for. Why should we bother scrimping and saving for a future that I no longer believed in? My life had effectively ended. Nothing had any value any more.

It was over. Period.

The End of Life

To put this bluntly, apathy is the death of a life. Of your life. Of all that you used to take for granted, and that has now passed.

What you were, what you have been, has died.

There is no future. There is nothing. Until you experience some kind of resurrection, some beginning of new life.

This is, therefore, a time of utter aimlessness, of inability to focus on anything. People who have retired unwillingly, or who have been fired, experience this. They fritter their time away, doing nothing, accomplishing nothing.

Donna Hohmann Ewy and Rodger Frank Ewy state that
mothers who have lost an unborn child through miscarriage or stillbirth have the same feeling: "Bereaved mothers spend their days in restless, aimless searching for something to do. They may begin one thing and leave it unfinished to begin another. They are unable to start and carry
on any organized activity... Their lives have lost meaning."
(*Death of a Dream*, Dutton Signet/Penguin, 1984, p. 71, 80)

During this period of apathy, people do things they may
later regret. After my mother died, my father gave away many
items that the two of them had once treasured. China, cutlery,
vases, pitchers – once-valued mementos left the house in a never
ending stream. Years later, Joan and I asked what had become
of a particular blue vase, so bright it was almost luminescent.
"I've no idea," Dad said. "I'm sure I gave it to someone."

I've no doubt that Dad wanted to give people associated with my mother something tangible to remember her
by. Somewhere, someone has a beautiful blue vase. Every
time they see it, they say, "Mary Taylor loved that vase; we
loved Mary Taylor." But I also have no doubt that Dad gave
those things away because he saw no point in keeping them.
Without Ma, there was no future, no reason to retain things.

Journal entry   August 18

I am utterly dried up, emotionally. I don't cry any more. I
don't feel anything, except a guilty feeling that Stephen
can slip so easily out of our routines, as if he had just
gone away on holiday or something. I don't even feel a
great emptiness.

Grief does more than just sap energy. It creates an apathy
in which nothing matters any more.

Television, on slow-news days, will show pictures of refugees, of victims of disaster, gazing blank-eyed at nothing. They don't rail against injustice. They don't fight their fate. They don't even cry. They just sink into an emotional abyss.

I used to think of this fatalism as a religious response. Now I suspect it is more a symptom of shock, of grief over what has happened to them. William Sargant, for example, suggests that under extreme stress, people reach a state of emotional exhaustion. "Normally energetic and active people would sit about complaining that nothing interested them any longer." (*Battle for the Mind,* p. 87)

During this apathy, everything becomes equally important (or unimportant). Sargant, who did much of his research on war conditions, compared it to battle fatigue: "...normal people in periods of intense fatigue [report] that there is little difference between their emotional reactions to important or trivial experiences." (*Battle for the Mind,* p. 64)

Under "normal" circumstances – whatever that is – people are able to make distinctions. They can set priorities, evaluate risks, determine orders of importance. Sargant claims that, under sufficient stress, that capacity disappears. For the soldier under fire, keeping shoelaces properly tied seems as important as staying alive.

Sargant defined four levels of what he called "protective inhibition." In the last phase, he said, people lose all sense of proportion. Values flipflop; people grasp at straws; the unthinkable becomes a preferred choice.

On a small scale, our daughter Sharon experienced that loss of critical perspective. She faced the loss of a job she had spent six years training for. "I started wishing I could have an accident," she told me later. "Not a big one. Not a really serious one. But serious enough that I could be disabled, and escape from all the crap I was going through."

In her state of mind, the possibilities of broken bones,

hospitalization, even loss of life, seemed preferable to an intolerable work situation.

When you get to that point, your state of mind itself becomes a matter of concern.

October 12

Dear Stephen,

I've been sitting here working at other things and thinking that I should be writing you, but not sure what about.

Somebody said to me, when I was down at Church House recently: "You must be devastated by the death of your son."

I could honestly answer, "No, not any more." Sometimes those who have just heard about your death are more in shock than I am — I find myself feeling almost callous about my lack of emotion.

Several months after Stephen's death, when the woman called me from the Bereaved Parents' Association, I felt nothing.

That apathy takes a long time to get over. During that fall, an editing colleague lost her mother. One of our ministers lost her father. A member of our congregation, widowed just two years before, found herself alone in an echoing empty house as the last of her children left home for a job in a distant city. A dearly loved uncle grieved for the loss of his wife. Another of Stephen's CF friends died in hospital.

November 21

Dear Stephen,

I feel that I ought to be able to reach out, to offer all of them sympathy. But I feel strangely isolated. Withdrawn. As if I couldn't identify with their pain, let alone feel it.

I suppose that in one sense that is very natural. After all, if you've just burned your fingers on the stove, you don't feel much inclined to lay them back on the hot element. When you're hurting, you don't want to be hurt any more. It's painful enough on your own account, without opening yourself up to added pain on someone else's behalf.

There's also a temptation – I see it in myself – to feel that one's own private tragedy is the worst that can be experienced. That's comforting in one sense – it provides an excuse not to reach out to anyone else in their pain, because it can't possibly be as bad as your own. But that's a dangerous temptation. How can anyone know how much someone else is hurting? How can I possibly know whether Joan's sense of loss about you is greater or lesser than my own?

But without knowing, do I dare risk opening myself up to more pain, by sharing in someone else's? Suppose it really is less than my own? Perhaps someone who has lost a leg can console someone else who has scraped a knee – but is it right? Is it fair? Isn't that like asking heat to flow from the cooler object to the hotter one, or like robbing those who are already poor to support those who are better off?

And is it really sympathy if I offer it as an act of will rather than a spontaneous outpouring from my heart?

Sorry to dump all this on you. It's one of those things that happens as I try to sort out this new life you've launched me into.

The final paragraph of that letter to Stephen indicates that I had begun to recognize that I was starting a new life. One might expect new beginnings to carry some excitement.

But two weeks later, I still had no sense of anything but blah. And the blahs go on a long time. For some reason, I had been thinking of Christmas – perhaps imagining how difficult it would be without Stephen. I had nothing to say, but I desperately wanted to keep in touch, so I said it anyway.

December 8

Dear Stephen,

...The traditional date of Christmas is probably wrong. If the shepherds were out in their fields at night, it was probably spring or fall rather than winter. And I gather that Roman records of the decrees of Caesar Augustus suggest that a September birth is more likely, which co-incides relatively well with December 8 for conception.

The celebration of Christmas on December 25th is almost certainly tied to the Roman festival of Saturnalia, a time when the populace generally went wild anyway, and so a few Christians similarly celebrating a different event wouldn't be noticed — whereas if they celebrated Jesus' birthday in September they would be only too noticeable and subject to instant persecution.

It's also a time for hope, as the days finally start growing longer again.

It's only a couple of weeks now until that happens. I find myself hardly caring. Light, darkness, doesn't seem to matter much any more.

I think I must be in some kind of depression.

Disheartening as apathy seems to be, it's a necessary stage in the grief process. It's a time for giving up: giving up old ways and hopes, giving up a struggle too big to bear, giving up a fight to hold on to yesterday.

You are finally letting something die.

What You Can Do

If you find yourself feeling that nothing matters, feeling

completely indifferent to good and bad, present and future, cause and consequence, you're not sick, you're just grieving.

You can't conquer your apathy by an act of will. There is no cure for apathy but time. And, one day, the discovery that you do care about things after all.

That discovery can only come if you allow yourself to get involved in activities again. Borrow others' enthusiasms. Initially, someone else's causes and commitments will have to do; eventually, you will find that they matter to you too.

If someone you know is going through this "don't care about anything" symptom, you have a very delicate tightrope to walk. In some ways, you become the other person's judgment.

If, for example, they're "borrowing" your enthusiasm, as suggested above, you may need to be more altruistic than you have ever been in your life. You have to consider what's genuinely best for the other person.

It's all too easy to manipulate the other person into your own priorities. The grieving person may accede to your requests, because he or she doesn't have the energy to resist. You might talk her into joining you for a holiday in Mexico; you might persuade him to join your fund-raising committee. But if the holiday isn't the kind she would have chosen for herself, she may feel later that she was taken advantage of in a time of weakness. If he loathes fund-raising, he may later resent your efforts.

Because inevitably, you will influence the other person. Just by being there. The alternative – far worse – is to abandon that person, to leave him or her alone.

This is not an enviable time to be close to those who are grieving. Their apathy will also dishearten you. It may make you angry. In the early stages of grief, you can hold them, console them, weep with them. In the later stages of grief, you can rejoice as strength and vitality and zest begin to return.

But in the meantime, you can only love them as you love yourself – and maybe more. Because they depend on you.

Birth Pangs

"After any major loss, you will be a different person... Your own new life will start almost imperceptibly. It probably started in the first few days after your tragedy, after something in you died... Somewhere, way down under the debris of shock, of pain, of loneliness, you will have started the labor pains of being born again."

Birth Pangs

Most of the books on grieving that I have seen end here. That is, they deal with the pain, the lament, the struggle of grief. Then they assert – explicitly or implicitly – that as the pain recedes, you're on your way back to being normal.

In fact, you will never be normal again. Not if "normal" means going back to who and what you were. Before something died inside you.

A minister told me about his marriage counseling sessions with couples. "Once you have been married," he reminds them, "you can never go back to being single again." You can get a divorce. You can walk out. But having been once married, you can never revert to your former state of singleness. You have been changed forever by your experience. You are now a different person.

Rick Hansen suffered spinal cord damage that left him permanently paralyzed from the waist down. Hansen was a fine athlete, if not necessarily a world class one, before his injury. He can never simply return to "normal" in the sense of having usable legs again. His accident changed him forever.

In fact, he may be a finer athlete and a better person than he was before the injury that crippled him. Had he never lost the use of his legs, would he have thought of driving a wheelchair, using only his own muscle power, around the world to raise money for spinal cord research? In his wheelchair, he became a goodwill ambassador for Canada in more than 50 countries.

His tragedy led him into new possibilities. That's the missing element, I believe, in other books about grief. They fail to acknowledge, let alone encourage, the possibilities of new life.

The Birth of a New Personality

After any major loss, you will be a different person. You cannot simply replace one spouse with another. Or dash from one failed cause into a new movement. Or bounce from job to job, city to city. Not if that former spouse, or cause, or job, meant anything to you. If they didn't, you had no grief anyway, so nothing has changed. If they did, no matter what you do next, the loss is going to leave a chasm in your life that you could not have imagined before it happened.

You may seem the same to your friends and acquaintances. But the landscape through which you travel has been irrevocably altered. And so have you.

Grieving is, in many ways, a sign of growing maturity. Those who have not grieved have not changed. Grieving is part of growing up. You have lost something that will not come back again. A friend, a spouse, a job, a status, an image of yourself, a loved one.

The question is not whether you will experience grief, but how you will respond to it.

Rick Hansen could have spent the rest of his life feeling sorry for himself. He could have used his injury as an excuse to avoid accepting challenges. He could have come out of the experience a lesser person than he had been. He could have handicapped himself. To his credit, he didn't.

Your own new life will start almost imperceptibly. It probably started in the first few days after your tragedy, after something in you died.

The first days after Stephen died, just dealing with the death arrangements took all our energy. People came to visit and to weep with us. We had to see funeral directors about his cremation, lawyers and bank managers and insurance companies about his estate, our minister and music director about his memorial service. We had no time, no stamina, for anything else.

When we took flowers to the nursing staff of his hospital ward, to thank them for the care they had taken of him, we were still dealing with the past.

When we drove up to the summer camp that had been a second home to him, we were still looking back.

My notes of those days are sketchy and incoherent, but I think that on Monday, both Joan and I returned to work. My office was in the basement of our house, so I had no escape from Stephen's ghost.

His therapy equipment sat on the floor in the basement. The striped chesterfield he often napped on, the exercise cycle he tried to keep in shape on – I had to pass them all to get to my desk and my computer.

I had been putting off that task. But at some point that morning, I said to myself: "I can't indulge myself in pity forever. Other people also need me. I'd better get something done."

The work I was doing had no meaning to me. My life had no meaning. But life was no longer on hold. Somewhere, way down under the debris of shock, of pain, of loneliness, I had started the labor pains of being born again.

The Rest of the World Hasn't Changed
Life goes on. That's the first, very small, discovery that heralds the way out of grief.

That discovery is often also a shock. After my mother died, my father and I found that there was nothing in the refrigerator for us to eat. We went out to buy some bread, some milk, some sliced meat, a head of lettuce. We were taken aback to find the supermarket filled with people, going about their normal lives as if nothing had happened. One shopper even had her hair in lime-green curlers.

Somehow, we expected the store to have dimmed its lights. We expected people to walk around in a hush. Because my mother, Dad's wife, had died that morning. I found the lime-green curlers offensive!

Someone else told me about her father dying during the night, in London. She described how appalled she was, the next morning, to have the garbage trucks come around, clanging the cans under her window.

And a man was surprised to find the trains still running.

Life goes on. And so do we.

A Process of Recovery

I like this advice from Harriet Sarnoff Schiff: "We rarely think of mourning as a process of recovery! But indeed that is what it is. You may hurt. No, you *will* hurt. But without the process of mourning, there can be no recovery." (*Living Through Mourning,* p. 78)

We have been maimed. Emotionally, intellectually, psychologically, we cannot function as we used to, any more than we could if we had lost a limb, or had a massive stroke. And just as a stroke or accident victim has to learn all over again how to function adequately, so do those whose loss is less physical. We have to learn again how to function without someone, something, from which we could not imagine ourselves being separated.

Harriet Sarnoff Schiff offers this advice to widows:

Even if you worked all the years of your marriage, that world will look different once you are widowed.

You became a widow through no choice or action of your own. That is a tragedy. By not acting or becoming involved you are furthering a tragedy for yourself. Although you were not widowed by choice, how you function as a widow is certainly a choice. (Living Through Mourning, *p. 60*)

That's the key point – you have a choice.

In the beginning, you are helplessly carried along by a torrent of events over which you seem to have little or no control. As time passes, you may still find you have little control over events. But you will have increasing control over yourself. Unlike the butterfly, you *can* influence the kind of person who will eventually emerge from the cocoon of grief.

Emerging from the Cocoon

I hesitate to call the change that happens either resuscitation or resurrection, though there are elements of both involved.

Folklore is filled with stories of resuscitation. For those in the Christian tradition, one of the best known stories tells of Jesus raising his friend Lazarus from the tomb. That was not a resurrection. Whatever happened to him during his days underground, Lazarus did not return immortal. He came back in the same body he had occupied before his burial. He would still have to die again, someday.

Recovery from grief is more than resuscitation. If grief could be dealt with as externally as paramedics giving a drowning victim artificial respiration, we could simply administer drugs, or exercises, or psychiatric treatment, to cure it, to restore us to "normal."

But neither is the emergence a resurrection. The Christian tradition usually refers to that word with capital letters – The Resurrection. Unless the Bible records were deliberately distorted, unless his disciples later went cheerfully to their deaths for the sake of a story they knew to be a lie, Jesus was certifiably dead when a group of friends took him down off the cross and sealed him into a stone tomb.

Two days later, by our manner of counting, he was no longer dead. He appeared to a woman, Mary of Magdala. He appeared to two disciples walking along the road to the village of Emmaus, and then twice to the disciples gathered behind locked doors, and then, apparently, to a considerable number of people over a period of seven weeks.

But although he had the same personality they had

known before his death, he clearly did not have the same body. He had a body that wanted to be fed; he asked for food and drink. It was a body with substance; he could invite Thomas, the doubting one, to feel his wounds. It was a body that could do normal things; it cooked fish over a fire, on the shores of a lake. But it was apparently also a body that could pass through locked doors, and that could levitate. It was the same, and it was different.

From one perspective, that's not a bad description of what happens to the person emerging from grief. You are the same person, with the same memories, the same abilities. But you are different. You see the world a different way, and it is a different world that you see.

Yet grief is not a resurrection either. Jesus did not have to face death again. Your experience has not freed you from experiencing more deaths, more tragedies.

No Return to the Womb

Personally, I think that the closest analogy to the grief experience is birth.

Usually, we hear about birth only from the mother's point of view. We hear about the agony of labor, the joy of delivery, of holding a newborn child, of having it instinctively nuzzle for a nipple.

But consider how traumatic birth must be, from the baby's point of view.

You're warm and comfortable and fed. You live in a familiar and weightless environment, where your every need is looked after.

Then one day, everything changes. An earthquake convulses your increasingly cramped world. You are squeezed through a narrow opening like toothpaste out of a tube. It crushes your head, your shoulders. You can't breathe; you're asphyxiating in this strange substance called air.

In the first few seconds, you have to learn to breathe. You discover the power of gravity that will continue to affect you for the rest of your life. You're cold; you need external warmth for the first time.

Over the days, weeks, months that follow, equally traumatic changes occur. The pain of teeth puncturing through tender gums. The effort to raise first limbs, then a whole body, against the unfamiliar tug of gravity. To learn to crawl, to walk. Falling down, and hurting yourself, and getting up and trying again. The frustration of being unable to express your needs, your feelings, except through floods of tears. Learning how to communicate, to shape words to suit your situation.

The new life of a baby does not come easily. Every step has to be learned. There are no precedents to pick up on, no long-held habits to fall back upon.

Grief is like that. Normal, for a newborn baby, was the womb. A baby does not return to normal after its birth; it cannot go back to the womb. Instead, it launches a new life, a life that it could not have imagined before it was born. And this strange new life becomes a different "normal."

That's a perfect description of grief. You cannot go back to your previous life – even if it does seem, in hindsight, as attractive as the womb must to a newborn baby. You have no choice but to go ahead and adapt to your new situation.

Some babies learn to deal with this new life much more effectively than others. Some people learn to deal with their new life more effectively than others. That's the nature of grief. In this new world, you advance tentatively, feeling your way every step. You fall down, and get hurt all over again. But you can't stay there crying, so you get up and try again.

It's certainly not a world you wanted to find yourself in. Often, it's a world we would have given anything to have avoided. And I do mean anything. During Stephen's dying days, I would cheerfully have given up my own life – I would have given him any of my organs, I would have pitched myself out of the hospital window – if I really believed it would let him live.

"I am a more sensitive person, a more effective pastor, a more sympathetic counselor because of Aaron's life and death than I would ever have been without it," writes Rabbi Harold S. Kushner in *When Bad Things Happen to Good People*. "And I would give up all of those gains in a second if I could have my son back. If I could choose, I would forego all the spiritual growth and depth which has come my way because of our experiences..." (pp. 133–34, 264)

What You Can Do

There are no clear destinations in this strange new world. I cannot tell you where you will go, or when you will arrive there. I can only point you towards some route markers that will help you to measure your own progress. Some of those you have already encountered in the previous chapters. As you identify the symptoms of grief in your own experience, you will have a sense of how you are moving through them.

There are a number of additional clues to help you trace your progress in the transition to new life. I deal with these in greater detail in the chapters that follow.

Habits

Your body always tells you the truth. It doesn't know how to lie. The things your muscles and limbs do without your conscious volition will tell you a great deal about how much you are still a prisoner of the past.

Dreams

Your dreams will probably become considerably more vivid during grief. If you pay attention to them, they will tell you a lot about your state of mind. You don't need an expert to help you interpret your dreams; what matters is an awareness of the way in which your dreams are changing.

Images

When you talk about your grief, you will inevitably resort to certain metaphors to describe your experience. Pictures will spring unbidden to your mind, to help you make sense of your situation. Pay some attention to them; as those pictures evolve, you will see how you too are changing.

The Search for Meaning

You will ask "Why me?" (Or "Why him?" "Why her?") As time passes, you will begin to formulate some answers. Bit by bit, pieces of the puzzle will fall into place. The answers may never be fully satisfactory. But they will become answers that you can at least live with. The gradual evolution of those answers is another clue to your healing.

Habits

Your mind can lie to you. Your emotions can mislead you. But your body always tells you the truth.

Time and time again, I told myself that I was doing just fine. I was recovering from Stephen's death. I was not incapacitated. I could handle my writing and editing assignments quite well, thank you. I really thought that was true.

My emotions seemed to be under control. I did not have tears suddenly welling up, like an artesian well out of control. I could discuss Stephen without breaking down.

But my body betrayed me. It was accustomed to certain habits, and it continued to perform those habits. So did Joan's body.

> September 12
>
> Dear Stephen,
>
> The house is empty. Before Joan came to bed last night, she went into both of your rooms, yours and Sharon's, just to check them.
>
> When you were younger, we always went into your room to kiss you goodnight. You never stirred; you slept so peacefully. But when we told you about it, later, you said it made you feel warm inside to know it.
>
> The old reflexes still hold.

For years, Stephen was my hiking partner. I became a Scout leader because of him. He found the weekly Scout meetings a bit of a bore. But four, five, sometimes six times a year, we went camping. He lived for those weekends.

In the beginning, I guided him in choosing camping and hiking equipment. But soon, his knowledge surpassed mine. He gathered the catalogs and haunted the sporting goods stores. He talked with experts and learned to distinguish the valuable products from the gimmicks.

When camping catalogs and magazines arrived in the mail, we jointly went over them to see if there was something new, something we needed for our next camping trip.

November 9

Dear son,

I am not doing as well as I thought.

This morning, your catalogue arrived from the Goolak Backwoods Co-op. A big fat catalogue, filled with wonderful bits of camping equipment — new tents, lightweight stoves, improved packs that can be slung onto airline conveyor belts without self-destructing at the first corner.

I found myself flipping through the pages, and thinking, "That's nice, I'd like that. I could use that."

Then, like an icicle stabbing my heart, I heard myself also asking the question, "Why? What good is it now?"

The fact is that we were a team, you and I. I got upset with you, sometimes, if you didn't seem to be pulling your weight in cooking or gathering firewood or whatever. But in spite of that, we got along well together on camping trips. It was a time of closeness for us.

Habits, unfortunately, don't die as easily as people. I know you are dead. I know we aren't going camping together any more. But something inside me still doesn't believe it, and so I look through the catalogue with hope, with expectation.

Until that voice asks, "Why?"

Other habits trip up other people.

Widows, I'm told, frequently continue to turn down their husband's side of the bed, and put his pyjamas under his pillow. The familiar routine may be valuable during the "wallowing" stage of grief. But at some point, the routine loses any value. Then it's time to build some new habits, some new routines.

There is only one way of breaking those traitorous habits. That is to replace them with new ones. Your muscles and your reflexes need retraining.

"Going out shopping for the groceries alone can be an ordeal," advises Michael A. Simpson. "Making the change more complete could help. Try a different store, a different day or time, and go with a friend. When it seems very hard to decide what to do first, maybe it's not so important where you start, so long as you start. Choose a simple task and get started." (*The Facts of Death*, p. 252)

By establishing new habits, you counteract that feeling of helplessness, that feeling of being a piece of flotsam whirled along by an uncontrollable torrent.

What You Can Do

Don't make dramatic changes, like selling your house or moving to Mexico. Not yet, anyway. Focus on the little things you can do to remind yourself that life is different now. Sit in a different place at the meal table. Have a bath at night instead of your usual shower in the morning. Back the car into the driveway instead of backing it out.

Be cautious when choosing these acts. Don't decide to do something which will seem like a betrayal of the past. If you and your spouse enjoyed a cup of coffee together, switching to tea may feel like a repudiation of those good times you shared. But it may not make any difference to put the garbage can on the left side of the driveway instead of the right. Small as these changes are, each one is a victory. Each one asserts that you are not helpless, that you are not a victim of circumstances.

Each new habit reduces the likelihood that you will be suddenly, unexpectedly, betrayed by some old habit.

If someone you care about is grieving, there's nothing you can do. The habits belong to the other person, not to you. Only the other person can change them. If you insist on sitting where the former spouse used to sit, you'll probably just be resented.

Do what you've always done. Just don't do anything that forces the grieving person to perpetuate a past habit.

Dreams

If you're like me, you are not very conscious of your dreams normally. No matter how vivid they are as you dream them, they quickly fade once you open your eyes.

During the months after Stephen's death, however, I had extremely intense dreams. I could remember them clearly, and I knew exactly what they meant.

My dreams did not start immediately. (For some people, they never start.) As Elisabeth Kübler-Ross explains: "Real dreaming about deceased children usually occurs a few weeks or months after the death of a child, when the agonizing pain and grief are lifted, and the first quiet nights resume with normal sleep." (*On Children and Death*, Macmillan, 1983, p. 176)

But once dreaming started, it was like opening the floodgates of a dam. Because my grief focused on one person, so did my dreams. I dreamed about Stephen. Over and over again.

August 28

Dear Stephen,

I'd like to think of you sitting on a point of land somewhere, on the sun-warmed rocks, with a breeze off the water ruffling through your hair and murmuring in the leaves and needles of the trees, and the waves lap-lapping at the rocks near you.

I had a dream about that, not too long after you died. It wasn't any place that I had ever seen, I think. Nothing that I can remember seeing, anyway. Though it wasn't too unlike the rock bluff at Aunt Eleanor's cottage.

My first dreams about Stephen simply re-created the life we had shared.

As time passed, I began to realize that the dreams developed a pattern. I was reliving Stephen's life – working my way through the years, perhaps exorcising them as I went.

And so I dreamed that Joan was pregnant again – a most unlikely prospect, considering my vasectomy 15 years before! It may have been a desperate yearning to replace the lost child, much as families sometimes rush out and get a new puppy when the old dog dies. But I think it was more a rehearsing of my loss, a loss of memories that started with Joan's pregnancy.

In later dreams, I saw Stephen as a toddler, as a young child. Once again we danced along beaches, threw stones in the water, cut Christmas trees in the woods, built campfires, struggled through blizzards. None of these dreams happened exactly as I remembered them in real life, but I could recognize the emotional experiences in each one. And in each one, Stephen was a little bit older.

Until I reached the present.

September 18

Dear Stephen,

I dreamed again last night, but this time, in my dream, I knew that you were dead. Perhaps that's a good sign. Perhaps it means that your death has finally penetrated to my sub-conscious levels.

About the same time, something new started happening in my dreams. I didn't stop dreaming about Stephen. But I began to dream about Stephen in situations we had never experienced together.

September 15

Dear Stephen,

I slept in again this morning. Joan went off to work, while I lay there and dreamed. And I had the strangest dream – I do, sometimes, in those sleeps-that-come-after-a-sleep.

I dreamed that we were playing field hockey, you and I. On the field out behind Union College, in Vancouver, where I used to play field hockey as a university student. The field is gone now; it's been turned into a parking lot. You never played field hockey at all.

So it makes no sense at all for me to think about you being out there on the field with me, with the tower of Union College rising over the woods beyond, the sun bright on the grass field, the mountains standing cold and clear against the sky on the far side of Burrard Inlet.

One night, a dream told me, clearly, that things had changed.

October 5

Dear son,

Sometime during the early morning hours, I had another dream about you.

The setting was important. It was in the mountains, somewhere where a valley forms into a Y. It might have been along the coast, where tidal flats form in the deep fiords off the Skeena River. But I think more likely it was something like the Athabasca Valley, where the Sunwapta River flows in from the south, joining the main river valley as it comes down from the west, and then the two of them together flow north. It was a broad valley, lined with mountains, with a bright blue sky above and light fluffy clouds on the horizon. And the valley bottom was braided with stream channels.

The details are not clear. The only thing that is clear is that you and Ronny Mason were in a canoe, and had just pulled up by a sandbank. I came down to welcome you.

Ronny, as usual, was being the big-mouth, full of the pair's exploits and accomplishments. I got the gist of it – you had been up the side channel to a dam or a falls, you had then crossed to a point or a bay up the main fiord/valley, and completed the triangle back to where you now were. Even though the water was low and you had to walk or run the canoe up many of the streams, and perhaps carry it across some of the bars, you had done the trip in record time.

In my mind, though, all I really remember is you sitting in the stern of the canoe, your paddle still in the water on the starboard side, tanned, hair bleached in the sun, glowing with triumph. That picture is so clear in my mind it might be a photograph. Whatever it was, you had done it, and you were pleased with yourself.

I hope that is how things really are for you. Because that is how I would like to remember you. Always.

Part of every grief process is a desire to retreat, somehow, to a simpler and less complex existence. During a time of breakneck growth in our publishing business, my business partner, Ralph Milton, expressed nostalgia about the early days when, in his words, "We did everything ourselves, and we knew everything that was going on."

That yearning for the ways things used to be, might have been, is a characteristic symptom of grief. Thus, in your waking hours, you will wish for simplicity, for fewer complications. And in your sleeping hours, you may dream – and probably very vividly – about the way things used to be. I dreamed about girl friends in high school, as if re-writing history, as if wondering how life would have been had I married someone other than Joan.

October 19

Dear Stephen,

When I was much younger, I used to feel that dreaming about my girlfriends was a sign that I was breaking up with them. It usually worked that way, though I don't know why. Maybe it was that my infatuation was lessening, and therefore I could distance myself from them enough emotionally that I could afford to dream about them. Or maybe it was just that I was getting more emotionally upset about my relationship with them, and so they intruded into my dreams.

All of us, recently, have been dreaming a lot about you. Perhaps it's our way of distancing ourselves from you. I don't like to think of it as breaking up with you. But maybe in a way that's what we're doing.

November 4

Dear Stephen,

I dreamed about you again. Yes, I know, dreams, dreams, dreams. Yet they tell me so much about what's happening to me that I need to share them with you.

For some reason, I decided to check in your room. I thought I could hear you inside, puffing from some kind of exertion. So it must have been in the later years of your life, when any effort left you gasping.

And you were there. Your bed was facing the wrong way, so that your head was at the opposite end from where you usually had it. But you were there.

I knew you were dead.

I looked at you for a moment and wondered what age you were. Your eyes were bright blue and dancing. You might have been 15, or 17, even 19.

You asked, with your deceptive innocence: "Is something wrong, Dad?"

I reached out for you, somehow expecting this, even in my dream, to be a mirage, an illusion. And my fingers actually felt your skin, your plaid shirt...

I gathered you into my arms, and wailed. It was the same kind of wail that came out of me the morning after you died, when I called Bob and Marion in Burlington to tell them you had died. And as I hung up, involuntarily, I heard myself crying out, "Oh, Stephen, Stephen, I miss you so..." On that occasion, Joan heard, and came downstairs, and comforted me.

In the same way, she heard me in my dream, and came in and looked at me.

And I sat there on the edge of your bed, holding you. Except that I knew, from where she stood, there was nothing in my arms. Nothing. It's such a terrible word, such a terrifying thought. I knew there was nothing there. But I couldn't let you go. I couldn't.

In that dream, I remember, I held Stephen tightly, with my face buried in his hair, pressing my lips against his scalp. And when I woke, I could still feel the pressure of his skull on my front teeth. If I push hard against my teeth with my thumb for several minutes, for some time afterwards I can feel those teeth re-adjusting their position. That was what I felt, after the dream. I still have difficulty believing it was only a dream.

Gradually, the dreams evolved. They became less painful, more philosophical. They told me, in the language of imagery and action, that I was slowly coming to terms with the loss of a son. In ways I could never have put into words at the time, I was beginning to put the pieces of the puzzle together and gain some understanding of my new life.

November 26

Dear Stephen,

I had another strange dream last night. I can't remember the details — the story, if there was one, wasn't particularly important.

I was on a mountain, of granite, polished by glaciers and running water. And the whole story seemed to consist of going up and down that mountain. Down into a valley where some shacks huddled at the base of a dry waterfall. Up where a trail hung out over the cliffs with a view far off to where earth and sky joined together.

The first time I went up, I was a person. Once I had been down and went back up the second time, I was a ghost. A spirit. Someone who had died. It took a while for the realization to get through.

There wasn't any moment when death came — just as, perhaps, there isn't any moment when we can say that an embryo becomes a human being.

Perhaps I missed something significant. Yet I had a sense that I was no longer what I was, or what others around me were. But I still was.

I don't understand it at all. I don't think it was a subconscious death wish. All I get out of it is a feeling that death may not be such an absolute barrier after all. It may be much more transparent, more diffuse. Final, yes. But not like crashing through a wall or flipping a switch. A more gradual and progressive thing. As if life extends into death, and death starts during life, and what I normally think of as the end is merely an episode along the way.

I wish I could ask you what it was all about. You've gone on ahead of me. You know things that I will only discover years from now.

If, that is, death is not just the snuffing out of a flame,

the end beyond which there is no more. No more anything. Just nothing.
  I wish I knew.

I still dream occasionally of Stephen. Perhaps I always will. There's always a pang of pain when those bright blue eyes transfix me. Perhaps there always will be. But it's not as painful, or as often, as it used to be. In that way, my dreams continue to chronicle my progress.

What You Can Do

If you're grieving, welcome your dreams. They're both part of your therapy, and clues to your process of recovery.

Keep some kind of a dream journal, if you can. Dreams fade all too quickly. Writing down even a few details will help you to remember better.

Write down also how you felt in your dream, how you felt when you woke up.

Don't worry about understanding your dreams. They don't have to make sense. They are neither prophecy nor diagnosis. They are not glimpses into the supernatural, or into the great beyond – they are glimpses into you.

Over weeks or months, you will find your dreams changing. It's the changes, not the individual dreams, that tell you what's going on in you.

If someone you care about is grieving, ask about his or her dreams. Try to be interested, even if you don't personally have much faith in dreams. Do not try to interpret other people's dreams. The dreams are theirs, not yours. Merely talking about the dreams will help many people see patterns, developments, that they might otherwise miss.

So just listen. To the dreams, and to the person having the dreams.

Images and Metaphors

Grief is, at heart, an indescribable experience. We do not possess the words to express fully what's happening to us. We have to press the words we use for ordinary events to their limits to convey even a fraction of the reality of grief.

So, almost inevitably, we resort to imagery. (We have to do the same thing when we try to describe God.) We take ordinary things – sights and sounds, touches and tastes, even smells – and we say, "It's kind of like that. Only more so. Much more."

I have not encountered anyone – in person, or in my reading – who did not at some point create some kind of image, some kind of figure of speech, to describe the experience of grieving.

Private Images

We all choose our own images. The images you choose to define your grief will depend on your own experiences. Obviously, no one who has lived most of her life in the tropics is likely to choose the image of thin ice. Such a person might well, however, think of some aspects of grief as a hurricane.

You may find that one image dominates, or you may need to use a variety of images. You may, in fact, find that you switch images in the middle of a conversation, even in mid-sentence.

I have not seen this subject discussed in other books on grief, so I don't know what the most popular images are supposed to be. I can say confidently, however, that you will instinctively choose an image that allows you to express – to yourself and to others – your current state of mind.

A woman writing to Elisabeth Kübler-Ross thought of her grief as a wave. "It turned out to be better when I didn't try to fight the pain, but let it roll over me like a giant tidal wave and carry me along with it, until it spent its fury and dropped me gasping but alive on the shores of sanity. And like any storm, it gradually died. The waves crashed further and further apart, and somewhere, without my being aware of it, life became worth living again." (*On Children and Death,* Macmillan,1983, p.146-7)

Because grief marks a major upsetting of life, many people may have an image of a storm. In my letters to Stephen, I used the image of the storm only twice. Once, I contrasted "the thunderstorm of tears that used to over-whelm me" with "a fog that sneaks in off the water, blur-ring everything and then slowly condensing into drops that trickle individually out of my eyes."

In another letter, about three weeks later, I commented that grief no longer "hit me like a sudden thunderstorm of private misery."

Yet I suspect the image was more evocative than I real-ized. For years, I could not hear the familiar lines from Rogers' and Hammerstein's musical *Carousel*

>*When you walk through the storm,*
>>*hold your head up high,*
>>*and don't be afraid of the dark...*

without being reduced to silent tears all over again.

Patchwork Quilts and Thin Ice

I've seen other descriptions of grief as a patchwork quilt. People have no idea what kind of a patch each day will bring; some patches are bright, some dreary. But the patches together be-gin to make up a quilt. "Each patch is a moment," said a man. "You have to treasure each moment, no matter how painful."

Joan's most common metaphor was skating on very thin ice.

September 24

Dear Stephen,

Yesterday I was sitting in Don John's office at the church, and talking about how we were getting along. I suggested

> that Joan felt like a skater on thin ice – skating, managing, but terrified of cracking through and falling into the deep water underneath.
>
> Last week, Elaine Kaye came past Joan's desk. Elaine always showed a concern for how you were getting along, although I don't think she ever knew you at all. She walked past Joan's desk, and stopped.
>
> "Joan," she asked. "How is Stephen these days?"
>
> That did Joan in for the rest of the day. She said that all anyone had to do was look at her and she was in tears again.

Joan often fell through the ice. But in time, the ice thickened. She didn't fall through as often, and when she did, she was able to climb out again more easily, to recover more quickly from temporary immersion in deep grief again.

Katherine Fair Donnelly gives another example. A woman Donnelly identifies only as Charlene used two images. She described life as a path onto which the bereaved must step. On that path, she said, "What is originally a sharp pain gradually becomes a dull ache. That ache is there from time to time, but sometimes it is worse than others. It's similar to the physical pain of arthritis that may grow worse when it rains." (*Loss of a Parent*, p. 194)

The Tree of Life

One of my recurring images was of a tree. A tree that had a limb lopped off. A very large limb. It made an enormous scar on the trunk, a raw wound that wept sap down the bark.

> September 20
>
> Dear son,
>
> I'm beginning to feel like a tree that has had a limb cut off. The scar is still there. The scar will always be there.

But slowly I can feel the bark beginning to curl in around the edges, taking the scar into itself and covering it up.

I may never be able to cut a branch off a tree again without thinking of you.

As time passed, like scar tissue around a wound in human flesh, the edges of the bark would grow closer and closer until they met and closed. And then there would be no visible mark, except for those who knew where to look. But the scar, I realized, would always be there under the bark. The tree would know it, and would still feel the pain.

In time, the image of a tree opened into a broader perspective on life and on death.

December 5

Dear son,

Yesterday afternoon, I went out to the Voskuil's for a part of my church visitation.

We talked. They wanted to know how I was doing these days.

"What's the most difficult part?" John asked. His child-like curiosity sometimes overcomes his tact.

I had to think about that for a while. "Realizing that you'll never see him again, ever," I said at last, with the usual lump in my throat. "Realizing that something as important as your first child is over forever."

John saw that I was choked up, and so he started rambling to give me time to recover, talking about his philosophy of life. He thinks that we are like trees. We grow out of the soil, we take nourishment from it, and when life ends, we revert to the soil. Once a tree has died and fallen and rotted, there is no tree any more.

There is just soil from which something else may spring.

It's funny how that image of the tree keeps coming back. I thought of myself as a tree, when I was sensing the first traces of healing taking place. But I never thought of you as a tree. Or of others as trees.

Over the weekend, there has been an airline disaster in Spain, with 100 or so people killed.

In Lebanon, another refugee camp has been shelled, with many deaths. At the World Council of Churches, one of the most moving speakers was a woman from Lebanon who described sifting through the ruins in Beirut, and finding the pieces of a little girl who had come out to Sunday school for the first time the previous week. She was able to identify the girl's hand only by the teddy bear it was still clinging to.

Life is cheap, my son. All over the world, people are dying, just as you died. My grief is not special. For many of them, the grief must be worse, because their loved one's death came violently, painfully – through war, through starvation, through torture, through cold or disease or accident. I can't claim special status, just because I loved you.

It makes sense to think of a forest. When a tree falls, it nourishes the rest of the forest. When a swath of trees falls, through wind or fire, it opens up the forest for new growth, for grazing land for deer and sunshine for field mice. A death is a new opportunity. The cycle continues.

I just wish I could believe all that. Theories and doctrines and philosophies are for times when they really don't matter. If I'm not hurting, I can afford the luxury of playing with theories. But when someone you love dies, it leaves a hell of a hole.

Does the earth scream when a tree crashes, ripping its roots out of the soil? Does the forest weep that one of its number is no more?

I do. Because I love you.

Images of trees might not suit anyone else. But they worked for me – and that was all that mattered.

Life in the Pits

From reading and conversation, I suspect that the most common images have to do with holes, or pits, or chasms.

Sometimes the hole is a cave. "I had created a black hole into which no one but me was allowed to crawl," a woman told Harriet Sarnoff Schiff. (*Living Through Mourning*, p. 228)

A Manitoba woman said she spent several years at the bottom of a big black hole. "Sometimes I was looking down at me from the top of the hole," she told me. "I was very small, and the sides of the hole were very steep and very slick, and as black as tar. And sometimes, I was looking up from the bottom of the hole, and the walls looked as sheer as the office towers around Portage and Main."

Harriet Sarnoff Schiff coined some lovely mixed metaphors: "When faced with a seemingly bottomless well of fear and pain, far too many people begin to realize that no matter how much is done, it will never be enough. There is such a deep chasm that all the sands of the Sahara cannot fill it and make it level." (*Living Through Mourning*, p. 80)

Later in the same book, she added this one: "You may feel that God has turned his face away from you, or you may feel that there is no God. In any event, the end result is the same. At the same time you are most desperately in need of stability, you find yourself grasping at air. You are faced with yet another void in your life – not a tiny pinprick but a huge chasm that is dark and frightening." (p. 205)

It's easy to poke fun at such images. But the feeling they portray is anything but humorous.

For me, the hole, the pit, lay in the middle of a familiar path. I walked along that familiar path, doing tasks that I had done for years. I thought I was on safe ground, and then, without warning, I found myself falling, falling, falling…

December 12

My dear Stephen,

I keep thinking that sooner or later I'll get myself back to something like normal. But there is this enormous great empty pit inside me, an emptiness that you left behind. And I keep falling into the hole.

I used to wait for the hole to get smaller, or for it to heal over somehow. So that I could walk around without falling in unexpectedly.

That's not going to happen. Maybe never. The hole is just going to stay there. Normalcy – such as it is – will come only when, like a blind man feeling his way along with his feet, I have explored every nook and cranny of that hole, and dis-covered from experience every possible way of falling into it. I thought I was getting fairly good at tippy-toeing around the edges, but I've got a long way to go yet, I see now.

The hole inside me is part of being normal now. With all my heart I wish the hole weren't there, but it is. I just have to learn to live with that.

It's taken years. But I have learned how to walk around the hole.

What You Can Do

If you're grieving yourself, I suspect there is nothing you can do about your own images and mental metaphors.

The people who speak enthusiastically about "positive imaging" would probably say that you can deliberately choose healing images to think of, and thus hasten your progress through grief. I'm skeptical – both about the ability to has-ten that process, and about the wisdom of attempting it. I

suspect that if you try to deliberately imagine the hole filling in, the limb healing over, the ice getting thicker, your
grief will probably find some other image to let you know
what's really happening.

But if you can occasionally reflect on the metaphors
you intuitively use, you may learn a lot about your growth.

If someone you care about is grieving, pay attention to the
figures of speech that person uses. He or she will probably
be unaware of those images. But you don't have to be.

At appropriate times, you might be able to provide
encouragement by identifying significant shifts. The person who laments that she's *standing* at the bottom of a big
black hole may get quite a lift out of knowing that the last
time she used that image, she described herself as sinking
in the mud at the bottom of the same big black hole. The
mere fact that she now sees herself *standing* is a sign of
progress.

Meaning

August 28

Dear Stephen,

I just cannot believe – or perhaps I don't dare believe – that all that you were, all you had ever been, could be extinguished in that split second when you went from life to death.

The death of something or someone that you hold dear will launch you into the deepest search for meaning you will ever experience in your life.

The Rev. Dr. Harold Vaughan dropped in at the Five Oaks Christian Training Centre, near Brantford, Ontario, one afternoon. For several hours, he sat in the Centre's dining room, regaling the staff with stories of his life.

Two days later, he had a heart attack and died.

"Somehow he knew his time was ending," commented George Hermanson, Five Oaks' director. "And so he came out here, and spent that afternoon putting the pieces of his life together in a way that made sense to him."

Harold Vaughan had had several previous heart attacks, and enough surgery on various internal organs that I once kidded him that he should have his surgeons install a zipper. At the time of his visit, he was apparently in good health. But as George Hermanson noted, "Somehow he knew."

All people, in a time of crisis, go over their stories to find the threads that provide meaning. And the way you weave those threads together reveals how well you are dealing with the crisis.

Shattered Life

Initially, any major crisis will shatter your preconceptions.

Like a sheet of glass falling onto pavement, your polished philosophies of life will come apart into scattered shards. Some people never do manage to put the pieces together again. Some try to put them together as they were – and fail. Most find that the pieces take a long time to fit together, and they will only fit in a new pattern.

If you've been fired, you'll go over your entire career, trying to find out where you missed the boat.

If you've been divorced, you'll replay your entire marriage, identifying the places where it went wrong.

If you lost a limb, an ability, through sickness or accident, you'll find yourself dwelling on that accident or illness almost obsessively.

After Stephen died, I could think of little beyond the agony of his final days. The letter with which I opened this chapter continued this way.

Letter continued   August 28

You took one short quick breath. Then you paused, and gasped. And you were gone.

Just like that.

And yet, right up to that split second, if, by some miracle, you had recovered, all that you had said and done, all that we had done together and all those unknown things that you had done with others and for which they remembered you as I now remember you, all that would still have been a part of you. It could have been brought back. It could have been shared.

It was all still there in your memory. Going hiking. Carrying a backpack. Sailing a small boat in a storm, heeled over so it stood on its side. Riding a kite high over Lake Couchiching. Slamming a canoe through the rapids, or bending it around a slalom course. Falling asleep in the car, or fighting with Sharon over who had the most of the back seat, or stubbornly staying awake until long after midnight

---

simply because you had said that you would, even though you were only six. It was all there, still.

And in that fraction of a second, that immeasurable distance that separates one second from another, it was all gone.

But I can't believe that it is really gone. The experiences, the joys, the anguish, can't be wiped out as quickly as that. There is something real about those experiences and memories, that doesn't vanish just like rearranging the electrical configuration of the memory storage on a computer disc.

But where?

And why? Oh, my God, Stephen, why?

What was the point of it all? Why, if it is simply to vanish in the silence of a breath not taken, was it worthwhile teaching you how to rip a car apart and repair it? Why was it worth knowing how to light a fire in snow, or how to do calculus, or how tectonic movements create rift valleys?

The Unanswerable Question

Initially, of course, you don't ask a philosophic "Why?" You scream "Why me?" Or why *us*, why *him*, why *her*, why *them*? The personal pronouns reveal that you take this injustice personally.

Michael Schwartzentruber, like Stephen, has cystic fibrosis. Some two years after Stephen died, he approached me about publishing his manuscript about what it's like to live with CF. Mike had already been close to death several times; eventually, he would receive a double-lung transplant. His manuscript was, in many ways, an attempt to make sense out of the experience of imminent mortality.

He too had demanded "Why me?" But as he pointed out in his book, *From Crisis to New Creation,* no one really wants an answer to the question "Why me?":

I have found a provocative parallel in an incident in World

War II... The British were able to break German codes, and
thereby sometimes learn of impending attacks. On one such
occasion, the British intercepted a German communique
which detailed a planned air strike on the city of Coventry.

British intelligence was in a quandary. If they alerted
and evacuated the city, the Germans would guess that the
British had broken their codes. If they did not warn the city,
thousands of innocent people would be killed. But the fact
that they had broken the German codes would remain hid-
den, possibly helping to bring an earlier end to the war.

British intelligence did not alert the city. Many people
were killed... I wonder if the fact that Britain's leaders were
able to provide an explanation, a "why," helped the griev-
ing families? Maybe, if they were very patriotic, they could
understand and possibly agree with the reasoning behind
the decision. But I wonder if knowing or even agreeing helped
to heal the hurt, helped to fill the sense of loss. (p. 21–22)

Elsewhere in the same book, Mike wrote: "The cry –
God, why me?" echoes in the empty stillness of my soul.
Slowly, I realize that an explanation is not what I want. I
want to be comforted, consoled; I want to be held, loved."

The Evolution of the Question

Grief does not take kindly to easy answers.

As time passes, the question changes. From the plaintive
and intensely-personal "Why me?" it becomes a more generic
"Why?" Why do these things happen? Not just to me, but at all?

Why, for example, are there innocent victims, who did
not contribute in any way to their own misery?

Once upon a time, in the days of my own innocence, I
believed that we all bore some responsibility for our own
fates. Even accident victims, I thought, had the opportunity to take evasive action.

Stephen's death, and some other experiences, have
changed my mind. I now know that there are innocent victims.

Some people do become poor because of their own foolishness; many more are thrown into poverty by economic decisions made in distant boardrooms. Whole nations are impoverished by commodity pricing on another continent or by international power plays.

Some people become sick because they smoke or drink or work to excess. But someone who has cystic fibrosis or hemophilia cannot in any way be held at fault for their disease; it was given to them at the moment that a particular sperm cell penetrated a particular ovum. They were created with that disability, whatever it is.

Hemophilia means that blood won't clot properly. A minor bruise becomes dangerous internal bleeding. A bump on the head can bring on massive cerebral hemorrhage. Hemophiliacs need periodic transfusions of whole blood products to give their blood even minimal clotting ability. During the early 1980s, thousands were infected with the Human Immunodeficiency Virus (HIV) through those transfusions. Later, the HIV became full blown AIDS. In no way can those persons be held responsible for this further assault on their survival.

Howard Zurbrigg belonged to our congregation for a number of years, while he served the Canadian Bible Society. On a trip to Haiti for the Society, he contracted hepatitis, and received a blood transfusion. Along with the life-giving blood, he received the AIDS virus. Ten years later, while he was minister of Pickering Village United Church, while his congregation was overflowing with growth and vitality, Howard was diagnosed with AIDS. In no way can I hold him responsible for his death sentence.

Grasping at Straws

About the same time that Stephen died, a Korean airliner was shot down by Russian jet fighters. Everyone aboard the commercial flight was killed.

Inevitably, the papers were filled with human interest stories. Some of them penetrated into my private misery.

September 5

Dear Stephen,

I was reading in the paper today that Buddhists believe that people who die spend 49 days wandering before they find their place in the universe. At the end of that time, they settle in, to whatever they will be – a rock, a tree, an animal, or perhaps part of the Godhead.

When I read it, I realized that for some time I have had the feeling that you are not yet at home, wherever home is to be for you. You're in a period of adjustment, just as we are. Perhaps, when the 49 days are up, you'll find yourself settled in, and be able to reassure us, somehow.

As the end of Stephen's 49 days neared, I began to draw parallels between the Buddhist belief and the Christian faith I had been brought up with.

September 24

Dear Stephen,

Here it is, seven weeks to the day since you died. Ever since reading about the Buddhist belief that the soul wanders for seven weeks in search of a resting place – and thinking about the parallels with Pentecost, which was actually 49 days, not 50, and that 49 days is 7x7, the sacred number squared – I've been wondering if something was to happen this weekend, if you would, in some way, give us some assurance that you are okay, after all.

As far as I know, there is no connection between the Buddhist 49 days and the Christian Pentecost. My mental meanderings did not discover any profound truth. But the letter shows how a tormented soul will grasp, desperately, for any meaning at all. It doesn't have to be right. It merely has to provide a temporary lifeline through the darkness.

Bob Leland, the minister of a neighboring church, called this search for meaning "the ultimate question. It's the question that determines whether we believe in anything, or simply slide into nihilism or terminal cynicism."

In the search for meaning, we have a choice. We can believe that there is meaning, somewhere, somehow, in this tragedy, and we can search for it. Or we can deny that there is any meaning, and therefore not bother searching for it. One option is just as much a statement of belief as the other. If we believe there is no meaning, we will never find meaning. We do not, we cannot, start by knowing whether events have meaning or not. First we believe, and then we seek confirmation or denial of that belief.

I desperately wanted to find some meaning – witness my linking of Buddhist and Christian traditions! That search led me into some areas of thinking that I had not expected to pursue, and that under other circumstances I would probably have rejected outright.

October 19

Dear Stephen

I wonder sometimes if I am still writing to you, or if this is just me talking to myself.

Am I accepting that there is no more after death, that whatever you were, you are not any more? When your heart stopped beating and your lungs stopped breathing, was that all there is?

I can almost tolerate that idea now.

It's a painful and a frightening thought, that all we put into life may simply cease when death comes. When you lay there in that bed, you were still our son, even though you were not alive. It wasn't as if you suddenly became something else, something different. You were still Stephen. But whatever your memory held, whatever experiences you had known, whatever insights you had discovered, simply stopped being.

It's as hard for me to imagine that, as to imagine that beyond the universe there is nothing – a nothing that goes on forever and ever, because it is nothing. We can't imagine nothing. We keep creating boundaries and limits and things, because trying to imagine what nothing is like leads us toward insanity. So perhaps we think, for our sanity, that beyond death there is something.

But maybe there is nothing but nothing.

In Christian terms, I suppose that is heresy. Death is supposed to be the final enemy. Christ is supposed to have triumphed over death, and shown that it was not the end.

"O death, where is thy victory?" Paul wrote. "O grave, where is thy sting?" [1 Corinthians 15:55 KJV]

I just don't know.

Asking the Ultimate Question

Psychologist Victor Frankl developed what he called "Logotherapy" – that is, therapy by seeking meaning in experience. Frankl himself survived the horrors of the Nazi death camps only by telling himself that someday he would be able to tell his wife about his experiences. That conviction gave some meaning and significance to events that would otherwise have destroyed him.

Questions about meaning penetrate to the very basis of life, the purpose of existence. These are profoundly religious questions.

October 21

Dear son,

Last Sunday, at St. Andrew's United Church, John Sullivan preached about the man in John's gospel who was born blind, and was healed by Jesus.

"Who sinned that this man was blind?" the disciples asked. "This man, or his parents?"

"Neither," Jesus told them. "He was born blind so that the glory of God might be revealed in his healing."

That's a hard saying, Sullivan told us. It's a cruel saying. Why should a man suffer for 20 years, 30 years, who knows how many years, so that God could be glorified through him at some point? Why should he have to pay that price?

I sat there thinking of you. What was the point of the suffering, the pain, the distress that you went through? And why are some healed, and others not?

How is the glory of God shown in what happened to you? If there is a God. If there is any glory.

Now, ten years after Stephen's death, I can say that I accept the first part of Jesus' statement; I still dispute the last.

"Who sinned?" asked the disciples. "This man, or his parents?"

"Neither," said Jesus. That I believe. Stephen did not sin, being born with cystic fibrosis. I did not sin, nor did Joan, in being carriers of the cystic fibrosis gene.

But that Stephen had cystic fibrosis so that "the glory of God" might be revealed, I cannot accept. The gospel stories portray Jesus (mostly) as a compassionate and caring person. I cannot imagine such a person callously suggesting that the agonies of diabetes were acceptable if Banting and Best gained some glory from discovering insulin. Or that polio was okay, because it made Jonas Salk famous.

Was it fair for one person to live a lifetime of blindness, of helplessness, of social ostracism, to give God a moment of glory? So that some other people could be awestruck with wonder? I prefer to attribute the second half of the statement to the imperfect understanding of an early church still obsessed with the conventional wisdom that sickness was punishment for sin.

Pious Platitudes

Confronted with the profound religious questions of life and death, the church too often comes up with easy answers – the platitudes of faith and scripture. Harriet Sarnoff Schiff describes two instances in which a minister or priest missed the boat. They failed to recognize the seriousness of people's search for meaning.

In one, a young girl whose mother had died railed at a "patronizing" response:

> *Damn it, you can't stay a kid when your mom has died... He didn't understand when I told him I wasn't there for platitudes. He just kept on quoting from scriptures that he thought would help. I needed him to tell me how in the world I was going to make it without Mom. I didn't need biblical references!*

In another, a woman in mourning visited her minister for comfort:

> *She went to his office and wept her heart out. Then she turned to him and in a simple, probably childlike way asked him, "Why? Why my son?"*
>
> *"Perhaps this was God's way of telling you to be a better person," was his reply.*
>
> *The woman has not been back inside a church since.*

(Living Through Mourning, *p. 116–119*)

Schiff is not alone in criticizing church personnel for trivializing the grief experience. This is from Michael A Simpson:

> *One family I knew were rebuked by their priest for their sorrow*

and mourning, for he insisted that this revealed their imperfect faith in the Life Hereafter. "Your husband is with God and the saints," he insisted. "You should not weep but rejoice." I am sure God forgave him for his lack of compassion and under-standing, and even of simple tact, but the family found it harder to forgive. Faith can be a major comfort; the trappings of faith can be used pettily and meanly by people of limited comprehension. (The Facts of Death, p. 237)

The few platitudes I encountered still fester in my memory. The Sunday after Stephen's death, one man said to me, with the best will in the world: "Don't think of it as a loss, Jim. Think of it as a release."

At that moment, I didn't want to be released. I would have welcomed nothing in the world so much as being able to return to prison, if that's what it had been.

Fortunately, few people offered platitudes or predi-gested answers. And none of the clergy did.

October 12

Dear Stephen,

The question that I still cannot fully face, I realize, is the one about meaning. What was the point of all that struggle, that effort, all that determination and willpower – yours, mine, Joan's, Sharon's, and indirectly, your grandparents who couldn't do anything themselves but supported us every minute of every day with their prayers and their concern and their own willpower at a distance – what was it all for, if it had to end in death anyway?

I can't answer the question. Yet I believe, as I think I said to you at one point in those final days, that it was worthwhile – a thousand times it was worthwhile. I just don't understand why it was worthwhile, or how.

If I had to do it all over again, I would, gladly. Because we loved you. Because you meant so much to us. Because you gave us so much in your wit, your enthusiasm, your joy — just that gleam in your eye that said you were flinging yourself into this wholeheartedly, whether it was learning to walk or solving a mathematical puzzle of some kind.

Why did I try to teach you? Why did you try to learn?

Why, if it was all to end up with you hunched over, gasping into the oxygen mask for one more breath, and one more, and one...

None... No more.

What was it all for?

Life-Changing Insights

Eventually, the questions about meaning return to the personal – but with a difference. The initial "Why me?" evolves through "Why do these things happen?" to "Why is this significant for *my* life? Why was *I* part of this experience?"

In the midst of all my anguished thrashing came some of the most stunning and life-changing insights I have ever known. They would not, could not, have happened if I had given up asking questions about meaning.

It started the day Ronald Reagan invaded the tiny island of Grenada, in the Caribbean. We heard the news on the morning radio broadcast. The announcer said it was not known if the Soviet Union intended to retaliate.

October 27

Dear Stephen,

Ronald Reagan is perhaps the last person in the world to whom I expected to be grateful.

Personally, I think he is senile, incompetent, bigoted, prejudiced, narrow-minded, decrepit, doddering, and possibly suffering from brain damage. He has brought the world closer to nuclear annihilation than any person in history. He is probably the only U.S. President in history who could launch a nuclear war and feel good about it.

In recent months, he has involved the U.S. armed forces in Honduras, Nicaragua, the Persian Gulf, Lebanon, and... You name it, he'll be there, waving a big stick and keeping the world safe for anticommunism.

Last weekend, it was Grenada. Because Grenada was building the kind of airstrip that every other Caribbean nation is building to attract tourist flights, an airstrip which every authority says would be useless for military operations... But Reagan is afraid Russia will use it for refueling or something. Why bother, when there are vastly superior facilities in Cuba? Why bother, when it would be further for Russian planes to fly to Grenada than directly to the U.S. if they wanted to attack...

Anyway, in the midst of all my fulminating, I started wondering how I would feel if I knew that nuclear war had begun. What if the only thing to do is to wait for death, either by missiles or by fallout.

How would I feel?

Would I throw up my hands and wonder why I had bothered living all this time? Would I throw out all the standards that I have tried to live up to all these years, and simply get drunk? Or go on an orgy? Or murder someone I think cheated me in some way?

No.

Why not? What would I have to lose any more?

Because simply doing the right thing is important for itself. Caring matters more than hating; helping is more important than hurting. Even if there is no satisfactory conclusion, even if my life were to end unpredictably in a nuclear holocaust, doing it right is what counts.

Suddenly, I realized that was part of the answer I have been searching for these three months.

Ever since we realized that you were dying, perhaps a year before you actually died, I have struggled with that question: "What was the point of it all?" Was all that effort, that struggle, just so that you could gasp a last breath at 11:17 p.m. on August 6th, too weak even to hold up your own head?

Now I realize that I was asking the wrong question. Whether anything was accomplished by your affliction, eventually resulting in your death, I don't know. I have to leave that question to God.

What counts is the doing.

I need to say that over and over again, to drum it into my mind. It is the doing that counts, not the accomplishing. Perhaps only God is capable of accomplishing anything, let alone measuring that accomplishment. Our job as humans is simply to do whatever we can, the best we can, so that accomplishment may be possible.

Conventional wisdom says that the end justifies the means. No way. It is the means, in the end, that justifies the end. Not the other way around.

The glory is not that you died in weakness and misery struggling to cough one last time. The glory is that you lived, that you enjoyed life and helped others enjoy life, to the best of your ability.

For us who have survived, the point is not that we invested all that will and dedication – yes, and anger sometimes – into keeping you alive and that we failed. No. The point is that we tried.

There would have been no chance of accomplishing anything if you, or we, had given up. If we had said, "What's the use, he's going to die anyway." If we had run away from the problem, as so many CF parents have.

And there would have been no chance of accomplishing anything if you had decided that you were going to die anyway, so you might just as well get smashed, drive wildly, dissolve your mind with drugs, or treat your friends and family like dirt while you enjoyed yourself any way you felt like.

But you didn't, and we didn't. We all lived as if life in all its fullness was still open to you.

Perhaps the key words there are "as if."

We lived "as if..."

Perhaps that is all we are ever called to do – to live "as if..." As if success were possible, as if the Kingdom of God were here, as if everyone could be trusted.

Because the glory is in the doing.

During that period I continued to lead a small study group on Monday nights – though whether I led them or they led me is an open question. The Monday night after that letter, we examined one of Jesus' more outrageous assertions.

October 31

Dear Stephen,

A theme from our study group tonight sticks with me.

Jesus made one of those remarkable statements that continue to baffle me: "Whenever you pray and ask for something, believe that you have received it, and you will be given whatever you have asked for." [Mark 11:24 *Good News* translation]

The confusion in tenses suddenly catches me. If you believe that you have already received it then you will indeed receive it. The past comes before the future. You have to act as if you have received it before you can receive it.

There's that phrase "as if" again.

In a sense, that's what we did. We acted as if you could have a full and normal life. And though in some senses you never did, in others you had more of a full life than many of your allegedly healthy contemporaries. You tried more, experienced more, took more control of your life, than some of them will ever manage.

That notion of living "as if" gave me comfort as nothing else had. It suggested that there might be an answer to the question, "Why?"

November 15

Dear Stephen,

This morning, I was reading a manuscript someone submitted to me, about the book of Job. The author looked at the philosophy of the three people trying to comfort Job, after he had lost his riches, his family, and his health. Their advice, however well meant, reflected the conventional wisdom, of their day and of ours. If you are righteous, God will reward you with prosperity and honor and comfort.

The TV evangelists still proclaim that false gospel. The assumption is that by loving God, by seeking God's will, people will be rewarded.

But in fact, the only reward for loving God is loving God. There are no other rewards.

If there were any justice, you should have been rewarded for righteousness. You weren't perfect, no. But you didn't harm people — with the possible exception of your incorrigible needling of your sister. You were generally thoughtful and sensitive, responsible and mature far beyond your years or your peers.

And what was your reward? To die in a hospital room

you hated being in, hooked up to tubes and oxygen hoses, feeling your mind and your will and your energy all slipping away. Until in the very end, the only way you could say you loved us was to take the last of your strength and put an arm around my waist as I held your head up so that you could clear the phlegm clogging your throat.

Three months later, it still hurts as much as it ever did. Does this agony never get better?

The only reward for loving God is being able to love God. In the end, even when the end is death, that's all that matters. I have to keep reminding myself of that.

By "as if" I do not mean pretense. If we had been pretending, we would have acted as if Stephen didn't need treatment, didn't need medication, didn't need any special care. If we had been pretending, Stephen would have died before his eighth birthday.

No, we knew the risks; we knew the hazards; we knew what could happen. But we refused to let it paralyze our family into hopelessness. We did not use his illness as an excuse. In spite of the sacrifices involved, Stephen did not become an invalid. We lived as if his disability did not exclude him from normal activities.

For me, the "as if" discovery was a life-changing experience. In a previous book, *Two Worlds in One*, I described how it changed the way I perceived others:

One day, we were in the narthex together. Big Art greeted some old folks arriving, towering over them like an iceberg over a dory. Watching him, I wondered what he must be like to live with. Did he drive his wife up the wall?

At that moment I realized she was watching him too. What I saw in her eyes, in that unguarded moment, was not frustration or anger or despair, but love. For her, he wasn't an oversized, overloud, heavyfooted embarrassment.

He just happened to have a few awkward limbs attached to an enormous heart.

When I tried to see him the same way, through the eyes of love, it made a world of difference.

The transition from death to new life proceeds slowly and painfully. Gradually, the questions shift from the past to the present, from what happened to what's happening.

As time passed, my thoughts spent less time in the hospital room where Stephen died, and more time on the experience of grieving itself.

November 25

Dear Stephen,

Last night, I was driving back quite late from a meeting in Carlisle, a few miles north of Burlington, in the inky blackness with not much visible in front but a small pool of headlight and an interminable series of other people's red taillights continuing to the horizon.

Almost inevitably, my mind wandered onto grief. I'm still a little bit baffled and concerned that it is such a selfish emotion. It focuses too much on my loss, my suffering.

For some unknown reason, I started wondering how I would feel if anything should happen to Ralph. Ralph is much more than a business partner for me, perhaps even more than a brother. Although we are like Mutt and Jeff in many ways, I simply could not do without him. Not at this stage in my life, anyway. It's as if he were part of me.

That was when the light dawned, to use the old cliché. The insight was so sudden and so unexpected that the highway felt as if it were bathed in light, like hurtling from a country road into the middle of a shopping plaza.

I realized why your death was so devastating. Perhaps it's why for most people, the death of a child is the most traumatic experience they will ever face in life.

The grief is so strong, not because you love someone else in *the same way* that you love yourself or *as
much as* you love yourself – but because you love them
as if they were yourself. That's why your death has been
so painful. I grieve for you because I grieve for me. I grieve
for that large part of me that died with you.

Because I loved you as if you were myself.

That's a whole new understanding for me of what it
means to love my neighbor as myself. I'm not very good
at it, I guess. There aren't very many people whom I
love enough to feel that if they died, a large part of me
would have died with them. I don't know how many
parts of me I can give up, so that they can be part of me,
so that I can love them as if they were me.

But I see now that it is possible. And I know now
what it is that Jesus expected me to do.

Thank you for that.

What You Can Do

If you're grieving, remember to look for meaning. Deliberately, intentionally, look for meaning. Look for it in newspapers, in magazine articles, in books. Look for it in your
friends, your work, your thoughts.

You may want to read books on grief and mourning,
like this one. Fine. But frankly, I do not think that is where
you will find the insights you seek. All you will find in such
books is the encouragement you need to keep seeking.

The meaning I found will probably not be what you
need. You may, in fact, come to the same conclusions that
I do – but you must arrive at them after your own struggle.
There is no other way.

Take nothing for granted; chase every idea to the ground, no matter how ridiculous or futile it may seem. First, you may find that this particular alley of thought does lead somewhere after all. Second, the intellectual exercise of chasing that idea will help to restore some vitality, whether or not you reach any answers.

I recommend keeping a record of some kind. I wrote letters. Years later, in those letters, I was able to trace my progress. If you can't write letters, keep a journal. Carry a small notebook with you, and title it "Insights" or "Discoveries" or even "Feelings." Put down a few words whenever a little orphan of thought tugs your finger for attention.

If someone you love is grieving, encourage their questions.

Don't attempt to give answers. If they wail, "Why me?" turn the question around. Ask, "What kind of an answer would you like to hear?" Ask, "What kind of answer would satisfy you?"

Above all, don't offer platitudes and prooftexts. A particular phrase from the Bible, the Koran, or the Bhagavad Gita, may have particular significance for you. Don't expect it to have similar significance for anyone else. It has meaning to you only in the context of your experience. First share your experience – then you can describe how and why this text matters to you. Then, perhaps, it may also matter to your hearer.

Similarly, do not belabor your own theories. Offer them, by all means. But keep it brief. A grieving person has a limited attention span. If the concept resonates with that person's experience, she or he will pursue it; if not, no amount of persuasion will make it acceptable.

If the grieving person comes up with outrageous ideas, do not ridicule them or put them down. Some of these ideas are straws, grasped for by a drowning hand. The grieving person probably does not believe these straws; but he or she needs *something* to hold on to. Help the person explore these straws, these ideas, with gentle questions. Remember, you are not the one who's drowning!

Starting Over

"I won't even pretend that starting over is easy. That's a myth, fostered by Hollywood... The former frog and the princess live happily ever after; the cowboy, his horse, and his girl (in that order of importance) ride off into a glowing sunset.

Things don't work that way...

We adults have long forgotten what an effort it must be for a baby to struggle onto its feet, and how many mistakes and disappointments must confront a child learning the complexities of speech. The closest we come to that realization may be in starting new life while grieving."

Starting Over

In the beginning, a grieving person is little more than a bundle of out-of-control emotions, like the storm-tossed surface of an ocean. There seems to be no pattern, no rhyme nor reason, to the tumult. But each lashing sheet of spray moves the whole mass of water a little bit. Gradually, those crashing waves of emotion settle into a rhythm. A pattern begins to emerge.

Somewhere in that storm-lashed surface, imperceptibly, a current of change begins to flow. Each wave contributes to it. The wilder the storm, the stronger the current that eventually develops.

In the Beginning

The first steps in starting life over again are always small ones. Very small ones – like learning to choose words that don't immediately reduce us to helpless tears. Whatever their value in healing, tears take a terrible toll of the energy we desperately need for survival.

Tentatively, we tackle the new tasks thrust upon us. Tasks that others find easy, we find almost impossible. Adults don't have to think any more about walking, about balancing on their feet; babies have to learn those skills by trial and error. Insurance and hospital administrators could handle with ease the paperwork related to Stephen's death, but it almost defeated me.

In our grief, we gain confidence – although it may be almost imperceptible at first. We develop new habits that better suit this new and utterly unfamiliar situation. Step by faltering step, we make progress.

To what destination?

I don't know.

Whatever the destination, it will apply to you, and only to you. You cannot know what you will become, any more than a caterpillar knows what it will look like when it emerges from its cocoon, any more than a seed knows what kind of tree it will grow into before it falls into the ground.

You will be what you have always been, what your genetic makeup and your social history have made you. But you will be different.

August 31

My dear son,

I suppose in time the immediacy of these constant memories will fade, and then I will start to feel disloyal, as if I am forgetting about you.

It won't be that, my son. It just means that like you, I have to go through the process of learning to grow up, to be independent, to live my own life. Gradually, as new experiences come along that don't have you in them, I shall find that I am not constantly reminded of you. The trouble is just that for 21 years, you have been part of every part of my life. That can't be erased, and it will take some time before it gets overlaid with other memories.

Light at the End of the Tunnel

The buzzword these days is "co-dependency." Co-dependency implies that each of us is in some sense dependent on others. We mold our lives to mesh with others. Sometimes that's unfortunate – when spouses feed on their partner's weaknesses to sustain their own worth, when unions and management define themselves by seeing the other as an enemy. Sometimes it's beneficial – when partners nourish each other's strengths, when a team of merely average players becomes a winning combination.

Most of us discover, in grieving, that we have been co-dependent. We gained part of our lives, part of our

192 Letters to Stephen

uniqueness, from a situation that doesn't exist any more, from a person who has gone.

During the spring of 1984, about nine months after Stephen died, I was a member of The United Church of Canada's national committee on Youth and Young Adult Ministries. For the opening of a weekend of meetings, we divided into small groups to talk about our goals and dreams for the coming year.

There were three in my group. The other two had some goals to share. And I suddenly realized that I didn't have any goals of my own. None at all.

All my goals had been tied up with Stephen. Things he depended on me for, things we hoped to do together. Disappointment when he had to drop out of university because of ill health. That desperate refusal to admit that he might be dying, because I was so afraid he might quit trying to live. Aching with the wish that he might accomplish some of his goals, his dreams: to drive across Canada, to hike the West Coast Trail, to see the autumn splendor of Agawa Canyon... I had no goals for myself.

That discovery was a shock. It was also, I believe, a turning point. I began, again, to seek my own dreams.

The Struggle to Find Hope

In the beginning, hope is almost invisible. In the torrent of emotions sweeping one downstream at such a breakneck pace, hope for the future is as impossible to see as the bottom of the river. But like the bottom, it is there.

Author Judith Viorst puts it this way: "In our own different ways we will have to pass through the terror and the tears, the anger and guilt, the anxiety and despair. And in our own different ways, having managed somehow to work our way through our confrontations with unacceptable losses, we can begin to come to the end of mourning." (*Necessary Losses*, p. 245)

No Magic Wands

I won't even pretend that starting over is easy. That's a myth, fostered by Hollywood – that if we could just free ourselves from the things that encumber us, life would be a breeze. The former frog and the princess live happily ever after; the cowboy, his horse, and his girl (in that order of importance) ride off into a glowing sunset.

Things don't work that way. The people in Nicaragua threw out the Somoza regime, the Philippines evicted Marcos, and Haiti got rid of Papa Doc. But life did not immediately become easier for them. Russia tore down communism, and Moscow found itself starving.

We adults have long forgotten what an effort it must be for a baby to struggle onto its feet, and how many mistakes and disappointments must confront a child learning the complexities of speech. The closest we come to that realization may be in starting new life while grieving.

November 30

Dear Stephen,

Perhaps I shouldn't moan. Even when I feel miserable, I can recognize some improvement.

Melody, your little Japanese nurse at the hospital, sent us some pictures of you at camp last year...

I cried over the pictures. But even as the tears fell, I was aware that they were a different kind of tears. They didn't hit me like a sudden thunderstorm of private misery, with those gut-wrenching sobs that start at the toenails and try to turn me inside out.

They were warmer. Softer. My eyes still puffed, and I had trouble swallowing, but they showered down more like a spring rain. I could smile even as I cried. Looking at you in those pictures, I could feel some sunshine through the rain.

Maybe there is some healing going on, after all.

Christmas Day

Dear Stephen,

… A while ago, I was sent a book of sonnets by a writer in Edmonton. Some of them are good, and some aren't to my taste at all. But in the last one, a few lines really caught me:

> Have no regret for words we have not spoken,
> for deeds not done, for dreamed of lands unseen,
> laurels unwon, past anguish, plans now broken.
> Think not with sadness of the might-have-been.

It's good advice, even if I can't always follow it. Of course I shall think with sadness of things that might-have-been, and I will wish that you might have seen some of those "lands unseen"; I'd like to have been part of your sense of discovery of Ireland and England, of the autobahns of Germany, of the lush islands of the Caribbean and the cliffs tumbling away under Macchu Picchu in the South American Andes.

But I can't. And that's that.

A physiotherapist, Athena Drewes, identifies four functions of mourning.

1. To accept the reality of the loss
2. To experience the pain of grief
3. To adjust to an environment in which the deceased person is missing
4. To reinvest emotional energy in another relationship

One can't, by an effort of will, simply close the door and start a new life. But one can learn to look forward, rather than backward.

What You Can Do

If you are the one grieving, there probably isn't much you can do. Simply dealing with each day as it comes along may be all you can manage.

The Chinese have a saying that a journey of a thousand miles starts with a single step. You can only take one step at a time. The seventh, or the seven hundredth, may be particularly difficult. But all you have to concern yourself with is the next step.

If someone you love is grieving, encourage that person to see the steps of progress being made.

A friend of mine took several years to recover from a deep depression resulting from blindness. Each time we met, I tried to tell her the improvement that I saw since the last meeting. It wasn't a conscious strategy – I simply hated to see her feeling hopeless.

Then one day, she helped me see what an important contribution I was making, even if unintentionally. "Thank you," she said. "You are my memory. I can't remember what it was like."

Whether you're doing the grieving, or the person watching someone else grieve, celebrate the beginnings of new life. It is not disloyal to discover yourself, and to let go of the past. In fact, it's crucial, if you are to survive.

Because each journey is so individual you will find your own way of letting go, of coming to acceptance of your new life, of learning to be grateful even for the painful memories.

For that reason, I'm not going to include a "What you can do" section with the following chapters.

Acceptance

I do not know when I accepted Stephen's death. Acceptance is, in a sense, the other side of denial. As unconscious denial gradually fades away, an unconscious acceptance of the death gradually grows.

The Final Stage

Almost all books on grief and mourning talk about acceptance as the final stage of grief.

The pioneering work by Dr. Elisabeth Kübler-Ross with people dying of terminal illness identified a recurring pattern of adjustment: shock, denial, anger, bargaining, guilt, depression, and acceptance. These stages provide a conceptual framework, but they are far from rigid. No two people will follow precisely the same pattern. Some people will never experience some of the "stages" – and some never emerge from some of the stages.

Kübler-Ross herself admitted that the stages were not carved in stone. Often, her terminally ill patients died before they had completed their adjustment to a starkly altered reality. Some were still angry, some depressed.

But when patients did reach some kind of acceptance, the effect was clearly evident. When my mother was dying of cancer, her weekly letters became uncharacteristically peevish, even whiny at times. And then, one day, those same letters almost shone. They had a kind of tranquillity, a peace, that told us she had accepted what was happening to her.

Not an Emotional High

Yet there's a lot of misunderstanding about that word "acceptance." Acceptance "should not be mistaken," says Kübler-Ross, "for a happy phase." She describes it as "almost void of feelings" – a time when the struggle is finished.

The description fits the grief process of survivors, too. Several authors prefer the term "completion of mourning" to "acceptance."

"Starting with shock, and making our way through this phase of acute psychic pain, we move toward what is called the 'completion' of mourning," says Judith Viorst. "Although there will still be times when we weep for, long for, miss our dead, completion means some important degree of recovery and acceptance and adaptation." (*Necessary Losses*, p. 245)

Harriet Sarnoff Schiff agrees: "Acceptance is the net result of a healthy grief process. It is the ability to recall one's special person without pain. Acceptance does not proceed from a denial of death but rather through confronting the event." (*Living Through Mourning*, p. 21)

Grief does not end suddenly, like the sun breaking through the clouds, or like having your car repaired, or coming up to breathe after swimming underwater. It's more like realizing that your car is never going to run like new again – and you don't expect it to, any more.

It's an odd sort of feeling, because it has no sense of triumph or accomplishment. Just acceptance.

And That's Okay Too

Somebody said that you've reached the "completion of mourning" when you wake up, and your loss is no longer the first thing on your mind.

I think that's too soon. I woke up some mornings with a writing deadline on my mind, or an appointment to meet someone. But I was not over my grief, by any means.

Acceptance came more gradually. Rather than no longer having Stephen on my mind when I woke up, it came when I could do things without thinking he needed to be part of them.

And that awareness started, paradoxically enough, with

one of Stephen's favorite occupations: hiking. I can probably illustrate that state of mind no better than by this letter.

October 14

Dear Stephen,

Bob Little and I went hiking on the Bruce Trail today, that
section down at St. Catharines that you and I have tried
several times to cover before.

Bob and Marion and the kids were here for Thanksgiving dinner. After supper, Bob suddenly said: "You got
any hankering to head up to Algonquin Park or some
place like that, Jim?"

No, not Algonquin. Too cold and too wild this time
of year. Besides, it's a long way.

"How about going for a hike," he suggested. "Is there
any place around here you can think of?"

I suggested perhaps the Bruce Trail. It seemed to me
that at this time of year, the color should be fairly good
and the weather tolerable on that stretch leading up to
Balls Falls. That's the one that we went to with the Venturers first, and got solidly rained out. Then, when you
were in Grade 12, I think, you tried again to go on a hike
organized by the students' council. But when the day came,
it was pouring rain again.

For a while I thought that nemesis had struck again.
Yesterday, the weather office spoke of a severe rain warning throughout this area. Sure enough, at three o'clock,
there was a most tumultuous thunderstorm which continued until about six!

But we went today anyway. There was supposed to be a
60% chance of rain today, but we didn't get so much as a
drop. For a couple of half-hour periods, the sun hid behind
heavy brooding clouds, threatening rain. But the rest of the
time, we had sunshine lancing down through the treetops.

The shadowed part of the scene made the light, when it struck the changing colors of the leaves, much brighter and more vivid. Bob stopped several times, his breath taken away by the beauty of the sunlight illuminating patches of rusty leaves along the path.

We passed through one section of sumacs, turning flame red. With a howling wind out of the southwest making the leaves dance straight out, it was almost as if the branches were on fire, and every leaf a tongue of flame.

There are a couple of spectacular little waterfalls. One is completely hidden by the woods. Unless you walk the trail, you would never know it was there. You wouldn't even find it if you took a shortcut across a switchback in the trail. But it has about a 20 foot drop, a delicate lacy veil of water running in slow motion over a lip into a silent and moss-covered bowl of limestone.

When we stopped for lunch, cooked on your little Optimus stove, Bob commented that even if the rain did come and we got soaked, the day had been worth it.

In the six hours or so that we were hiking, I found myself often thinking that yes, you would have enjoyed that section of the trail if you had managed to make it. And yes, there was a sense in which I wanted to hike that section for the two of us. But I never once felt that the day was ruined because you couldn't be there with me and Bob.

I'm almost pleased about that. I think that perhaps, at last, I'm learning to live my own life again.

I miss you. Maybe I'll never get over that feeling. I think about it and I get a lump in my throat all over again. But I know, after today, that it is possible to carry on without you. That's a discovery I needed to make.

Love,

your Dad.

Letting Go

We all have to let go, sooner or later. We let go of our children, as they grow up. Of our employment, as we grow older. Of friends and associates, as they (or we) move away.

Letting go is also a necessary part of death – the death of a person, a dream, a cause, a job. Sooner or later, we have to let go of the past.

Sometimes letting go after a death is harder than letting go in life. You can let go of an adult child, while still anticipating many more opportunities for contact, perhaps for a more equal relationship than in the past. But to let go after a death is to give up hope.

And that's always hard.

Judith Viorst has done some philosophizing on this theme: "I've learned that in the course of our life we leave and are left and let go of much that we love. Losing is the price we pay for living. It is also the source of much of our growth and gain." (*Necessary Losses*, p. 326)

The Urgency of Remembering
I had no idea, when Stephen died, how important letting go would become. In fact, I thought the exact opposite. All my energies were focused on not letting go, on remembering.

But "recovering doesn't mean they have to forget," says Katherine Fair Donnelly. "Nor does it mean they may not have occasional setbacks." (*Loss of a Parent*, p. 30)

As always, in grief, realization comes with pain. After I dreamed about playing field hockey with Stephen, I wrote:

September 15

Dear Stephen,
Hockey is behind me now. I haven't played in more than

---

20 years, though I still keep my old boots in the closet just in case I ever get a chance again.

Perhaps the dream was saying to me that I have to learn to let go. I have to let go of field hockey, which I will not play again. And I have to let go of you, to let go of the dreams that there are still things that we can do together, even if they are done vicariously. I can't do things because I think you would like to be doing them too, or because you would approve.

I have to let go of you.

Are you, somewhere, getting mad at me because I keep hanging on to you as my little boy? Are you moving on, to some state or existence that I cannot imagine, and you're feeling held back because I won't let go of you? You used to get so mad at me, at us, when we felt that you weren't old enough or mature enough to stay out late, to do things on your own, to make your own decisions. Are we doing that to you again? Still?

I'll take my old hockey boots and throw them in the Goodwill Industries Drop Box later today.

The physical act of dumping those boots symbolized at least a beginning of letting go of a son.

Starting to Say Goodbye

Several translations of the Bible have Jesus telling Mary of Magdala to let go of him. "Do not hold on to me," says the New International Version; "Do not cling to me," says the New English Bible. Both imply that Mary could, by her longing, prevent Jesus from moving on. She had to let go.

The awareness of letting go, of giving up something precious, is often forced upon us by external circumstances. Sometimes it will be a move to a new location. Or a realization that you can't afford that winter holiday any more.

Or by as little as cleaning up the basement.

September 24

Dear Stephen,

We were housecleaning. Joan wanted to do something with the glory hole at the back of the basement. Her excuse is that she wants to find me some more room in which to work. But the fact is that she can't stand the mess back there.

I started with the workbench. And as I started to throw out some things, and look for places where I might possibly be able to put others away, I realized why I have been avoiding this small space in the house for the last while.

There is just too much here that is you.

This was our space, yours and mine. Joan and Sharon rarely ventured into it. They didn't know what the tools were, or how to use them. They didn't know why an old shaft and bearings had been saved, or what it might be used for. To them, it was just a clutter of junk.

But to us, the bearings were the basis for a lawn-raking machine, the sheet-metal the raw materials for a small wind tunnel, the jar of smelly fluid a reserve for bleeding brakes on the car. The scrap of wood was a usable sanding block. There's a story and a dream behind every one of those pieces of junk.

And the tools. I picked up the old hammer with the wooden handle and the red head. We never had anywhere to put it away, so it just sat there on top of the workbench. That was a special hammer. Bob Little gave it to you when you were about five, along with a child's carpentry kit. The rest of the tools were junk — they couldn't have worked on a cardboard carton.

But the hammer was real. You used it for years, until Grandpa Anderson died, and you got his hammer.

Wherever I put down my hands, your tools reminded me of you. More, they remind me of our hopes for you. Perhaps I am too much attached to things, but I know the story behind every one of those tools. The screwdrivers that came to our workshop from Grandpa Anderson. You always considered the one with the rubber handgrip to be yours. "Why is it," you would ask, "that you people are always using my screwdriver instead of your own?"

I can still go through the racks and the shelves and identify every one of them. I know where each tool came from, and whether it was originally yours or mine.

All through the years, those tools accumulated. Always I kept thinking that someday you would be moving to a place of your own, and you would need some tools to take with you. Once you learned how to do things yourself, you would never be satisfied to be helpless when a tap dripped or a fan belt got loose. You would want to be able to fix them.

So you would take tools with you.

I bought a second set of socket wrenches, so that when you bought a car for yourself, you would have metric and/or American sockets to carry with you in the car.

But where you have gone, you can't take tools with you.

No, I don't think Joan can appreciate how difficult it is to clean up this glory hole. She might, if it meant throwing out the pots and pans that she has been saving for Sharon, or giving away those extra sets of china, of stainless steel cutlery, of picnic supplies… to admit that the sheets and pillowcases and linens that make up a trousseau will never be used.

It's very painful.

When I went to bed, I cried and cried again, for the first time in many days. There was salt in my beard this morning when I got up. I washed it out in the shower.

It was as if you had died all over again last night.

Perhaps that is what I needed to feel. Perhaps what I have been waiting for happened last night, when I dropped the old red hammer into the garbage bin.

Goodbye, my son. Goodbye.

I love you. I always will.

September 26

My dear son,

I realized, when I finished my last letter to you, that it was the first time that I had actually said goodbye to you.

On the night you died, as you lay there in the hospital bed with the pillows mounded up behind you, the light over the bed shining down on you, I knew you were dead. I had seen the pallor of death in your face. I had touched your skin, felt it cooling, stiffening, settling towards rigor mortis. Yet still, when we went out the door, I had a feeling that you would turn your head towards us and make some wisecrack as you left.

So I didn't say goodbye. I said goodnight.

I finally said goodbye in that letter. Then I realized what I had done, and I just sat there for a while.

Then I said it out loud: "Goodbye, Stephen."

I started to cry.

I had to say goodbye over and over again, rolling the words around in my mind, consecrating them with the salt of my tears as the sign of the covenant. That's what salt was, in the Old Testament; we discovered that in the Bible study last Monday night. It made the tears something meaningful, instead of just painful.

When it was over, I thought that perhaps I wouldn't be writing any more. Once you'd said goodbye, what else is there to say? There are no more words. That's the trouble with most departures — you stand there making small talk, putting off the moment of saying goodbye, because you know that once you have said goodbye, there is nothing more to say. It's time for people to get on the plane, the train, the bus, and to leave. Goodbye is so final. That's why we put it off until it is so rushed that we don't have time to say it properly.

But goodbye doesn't stop the caring. Even when Sharon has gone to Queen's, we continue to love her. Even when you have gone into death, we still love you.

Painful though the experience was, it was good for me to say goodbye. I realized later, when Sharon and I had a long conversation one night, that not having had an opportunity to say goodbye was adversely affecting her recovery.

Sharon had gone to Queen's University less than a month after her brother died. The excitement of getting ready to go to Queen's meant that she buried her grief under a pile of new interests. But as the excitement of university life began to wear, her grief refused to stay buried.

October 23

Dear Stephen,

I showed Sharon a poem that I had written about her when she was just three years old. We were passing through Smithers, on a summer holiday. There was a field in the middle of the town that had never been built up, and the grass stood long and clean in it. Sharon found something she wanted to show us. She came galloping through the grass wearing a bright red little nylon shell jacket, and both arms flapped up and down like a butterfly's wings.

I don't know why I wanted to show her that poem, at that time. Somehow, I felt that she needed to be reassured that she too had been loved, that we hadn't given all our lives to caring for and about you.

So we cried for a while.

I told her about the morning I said goodbye to you, and she said that she couldn't do that yet.

Yet for Joan and Sharon, too, the time came when they could acknowledge the finality of death.

November 17

Dear Stephen,

Joan was in tears when she went to bed last night. All she could say was: "I'll never see him again. I'll never see him again."

That's what gets me too, I guess. The utter finality of death.

When I called my father and Joan's mother, your grandparents, after you died, I said to them, "It's all over."

It's only now that I am beginning to realize fully what that means. None of us will ever see you again. It's all over. Forever.

Neither the First nor the Last Time

Letting go is a cumulative process, I discovered. I had to say goodbye over and over again. And each time, I realized I was still clinging to him, in some unconscious way.

December 12

My dear Stephen,

Okay, I give up. I thought that I might be getting along reasonably well, learning to cope with your loss.

Then on Saturday I was in talking with Don Johns. I mentioned something about going out west next spring to

> do something with your ashes. They're still sitting under the desk, where I brought them back from the funeral parlor.
>
> I don't even think about them. And certainly I don't think that they are you.
>
> "What will you do with them?" Don wondered.
>
> "Probably take them up to our property on Cortes Island," I said. "He always wanted to head back west again, sometime. We thought we'd go out and sprinkle his ashes somewhere, maybe on the bay – he and I had a couple of really enjoyable days out there."
>
> And then I heard myself saying, "It really should be a nice day."
>
> Now why should it be a nice day, I suddenly asked myself. Why not a pouring wet day, just as well?
>
> The answer was only too clear. Because I don't want to send you off on a rotten day. It should be a good, clear, sunshiny day, the kind you enjoyed going out in. It should be your kind of day.
>
> And it hit me. I still think that somehow you are around. I still haven't given you up.

Perhaps I have never given Stephen up. Perhaps I never will.

"It seems from what I have read and from the tears that I have seen shed over daughters and sons dead many years ago, that parents… may never give up grieving for their lost child," writes Judith Viorst. (*Necessary Losses*, p. 255)

But I do recognize that Christmas was a watershed for me. Late Christmas night, after all the guests had gone home and the rest of the family had gone to bed, I went downstairs to the computer to write what I genuinely thought would be my last letter to my son.

Christmas day

Dear Stephen,

Christmas, I have always believed, is a time for new birth, for fresh starts. There is something about the coming of the Christ child, as there was about the coming of the Stephen child, 21 years ago, that points us firmly to the future.

It's time for that to happen with me, too. I don't even know how to write this, as I pour out my heart to you, but I have a sense that it is time for me to let the dead look after the dead. It's time that I turned my attention to the living – to Joan, to Sharon, to Dad. Several times I have said that I have to let you go. Perhaps this is the time. Perhaps now, celebrating the entry of new life into the world, life that changes and transforms, I have to allow myself to be changed and transformed, and I have to let go of the old life that I have been clinging to.

So farewell, my son. Fare thee well. I hope that somehow, someday, some way, we shall meet again.

But if we don't – if this life is all there is and when we leave this earthly sphere there is nothing more – I just want to say thank you for having enriched my life so much. I love you. I won't forget you...

Thankfulness

A couple of months after Stephen died, my father told me: "Although it may be hard to imagine right now, there will come a time when you will feel thankful for the experience of having him."

I had no reason to doubt him. Nor had I any reason to resent his comment. He had been through his own grief – not just once, but twice. My mother had died in 1972. I had, by coincidence or good fortune, been in Vancouver at the time. I have a vivid memory of hearing my father sobbing in the bathroom. Dad has never been one to express his emotions very openly. Typically, his sobs were stifled, held back – so that he wouldn't inflict his loss on anyone else. On me.

I remember pushing open the bathroom door without even bothering to knock, and holding him in my arms. He had been trying to shave. The lather on his face smeared all over the shoulder of my jacket.

My mother had died slowly, of cancer. For some 16 months, she withered away. Dad nursed her, looked after her, watched her fade into a frail shell.

Four years later, he married again. And after six years, he again watched his second wife fade away. Her kidneys failed. She went through progressive levels of dialysis – at home, at a clinic, at the hospital. Eventually her liver failed too. There was no hope of recovery. They decided that they would not use any extraordinary measures to prolong life. Still, at the very end, Dad sat by her bedside trying to coax an occasional teaspoon of soup into her lips, to prolong her life by another day, another hour, another minute.

At the time, I felt an intense rage at God. It was not right, it was not fair, it was not just, I thought, for anyone to have to go through that twice. Once, perhaps. But not twice.

Just one year after that, Stephen died. So if Dad told

me it was possible to feel grateful, I knew that he spoke from experience. But at the time, I was still wallowing in misery. At any moment of the day or night, I would find myself back in that pale-green hospital room, listening to the breath of someone I loved becoming more and more labored. I could not imagine being grateful.

Grateful? For What?

I could not imagine thanking God for having had Stephen as a son. It still felt too much like a tragic waste: of our effort, of Stephen's promise.

Yet, when I look back over the letters that I wrote to Stephen, I can see that even in those first agonizing weeks, occasional glimpses of gratitude peeked through.

September 12

Dear Stephen,
We got a letter from the CNIB eyebank. It thanked us for donating your corneas.

It said that shortly after your death, those two corneas were used in corneal transplants. There are two people in Ontario today who are able to see, through your eyes, and who will be grateful to you all their lives.

I get all choked up, thinking about it. You always did have excellent eyes. You got so frustrated with us for our shortsightedness, especially when we were driving in the dark. You could sit on the end of the chesterfield in the basement, and read the writing on my computer screen. I have trouble reading it sitting in my typing chair!

But you also had a kind of special insight. You were often able to penetrate to the heart of a question better than anyone else. You were the one who made *This United Church of Ours* a best seller, when you suggested that it should start with chapter three instead of chapter one.

Characteristically, though, I shifted the focus from thanks to my own loss. So I ended the letter: "I really miss that gift."

During that terrible autumn, I still had speaking engagements to fulfill, commitments made long before Stephen's death. I could have canceled them, perhaps. I didn't. Perhaps I saw them as a way of dragging myself out of self-preoccupation, or perhaps I needed them as some kind of affirmation of my continuing value. And perhaps the reason is irrelevant. For whatever reason, I did them.

At these speaking engagements, I talked about Stephen. Not exclusively. But I did talk about him. In a sense, I felt I had to. I could not simply talk about discovering God in the ordinary events of life, as if nothing extraordinary had ever happened to me – that seemed like deliberate deception, like hypocrisy.

I have no idea how most of the people reacted to sharing the rawness of my grief. But a few, at least, found it helpful.

November 24

Dear Stephen,

A letter came in this morning. It was from a woman who had been in the group I talked to at Beamsville a week ago.

I think you might like to hear this. She writes:

"I walked in late to your discussion. I had just left my 15-year-old daughter at Toronto's Sick Children's Hospital to start kidney dialysis for the second time, having rejected a transplant. Your honest and open exposure of your feelings and Christian concerns during Stephen's chronic illness will always be an intense symbol for me.

"Thank you, and God Bless."

No. Not me. Thank you, son. Thank you that even after you have died, your experience – our experience – can be helpful to someone else.

It's a pathetically small return for all that you put up

with, for so many years. If you could have talked with her
directly, as you did time after time at the CF clinic with so
many troubled parents and families, I have no doubt that
you would have been much more helpful than I was.

But it's something.

It says that your value, your worthwhileness, didn't
end when you died.

Well done, my son.

Gratitude usually implies that one has somehow received
something. Not necessarily a physical object. I can be grateful for receiving a compliment, a hug, a glance of concern.

But sometimes, what one receives is much less tangible.
One time, when Stephen and I were out at a gas station, filling
up the tank of whatever car we had at the time, someone drove
in behind us. I seem to remember the car being a red Pontiac
Firebird. It had a flat tire. Really flat. Resting on the rim.

The Firebird's driver had never changed a tire. He
didn't have a jack. He thought he could just pump the tire
up and drive off. But with the tire separated from the rim,
he couldn't build up any pressure inside. So he stood there,
helplessly, staring at his own defeat.

Stephen and I dug out our axle jack, wedged it under-
neath the Firebird, and raised the car. We undid the wheel
nuts, removed the wheel, and installed the spare.

As we drove off, I felt grateful. For having received the
opportunity to help someone else.

It was that kind of intangible benefit that I began to
realize I had received from Stephen.

October 31

Dear Stephen,

On Saturday morning I was installing the storm window in the front storm door when something came to me.

I was standing there backing out the screws – and started thinking about the number of times we had done that chore together.

I remembered how quickly you caught on to the fact that a Robertson head screwdriver is easier to use because it's self-centering. It doesn't slip out of the slot and have to be constantly adjusted.

I remember how you learned to spin a screwdriver in your fingers. Some people never learn that. They keep turning the screwdriver with hands clenched around the handle, using their whole arm and forearm when they don't need to.

That's one of the things that I miss so much about you – your ability to learn things. Not big things, necessarily. But the little skills of life, like lighting fires and coiling ropes and spinning screwdrivers.

You see, when a pupil accepts something that the teacher is offering, as you did so often with me, that reassures me that what I have learned is worthwhile. It was worthwhile enough that someone else also wants it. That skill, that understanding, whatever it is that I have offered, was not a waste of time for me to acquire. By your learning it, my learning of it is affirmed.

I think that is one of the reasons that I miss you so much. You were my best pupil. No one else ever learned as many things from me. No one else ever wanted to. And so no one else ever made me feel so worthwhile.

Perhaps that's why I feel so lost without you.

Christmas is traditionally the time for giving and receiving gifts, a time for expressing thanks to one another. So perhaps it was appropriate that on Christmas day, our first Christmas without Stephen, for the first time I really felt gratitude for Stephen.

Ordinarily, our family has Christmas by itself, or with a few close friends. But that Christmas, sensitized perhaps by our own pain to the loneliness of some others, we had invited several other waifs and orphans to join us for Christmas dinner: a young family struggling through a separation and pending divorce, a man struggling to recover from alcoholism.

I was alone in the car. The city streets were dark and almost empty as I drove to pick up the recovering alcoholic. As my mind went back over not just the last few months, but the last 22 years, I was so overwhelmed by emotion that I had to pull off onto a side street to cry.

After everyone had gone home, in the wee small hours of Boxing Day, I put it all into a letter to Stephen.

December 26

Dear Stephen,

I realize now, as I think about Christmas gifts, that there was one thing I never did. I don't think I ever really thanked you for choosing us to be your family.

So on this Christmas Day, the first Christmas we have had to celebrate without you, I thank you for the gift that was you.

In a sense, you were a Christmas gift to us. I probably never told you this, but you were conceived one night in our first Christmas season as a married couple. We lived in the little house on East 61st Avenue in Vancouver. Joan's parents were visiting us, so we had to be quiet! We were a bit surprised by your conception. We hadn't planned to have a child quite so soon. But you were worth it.

There's no question that we resented your cystic